CW00393391

TEMPUS
Oral History
SERIES

DEEP SEA

voices

Herring girls in Grimsby unload salted cod, sometime between 1914 and 1918.

TEMPUS
Oral History
SERIES

DEEP SEA
voices

Compiled by
Craig and Jenny Lazenby

TEMPUS

First published 1999
Copyright © Craig and Jenny Lazenby, 1999

Tempus Publishing Limited
The Mill, Brimscombe Port,
Stroud, Gloucestershire, GL5 2QG

ISBN 0 7524 1836 X

Typesetting and origination by
Tempus Publishing Limited
Printed in Great Britain by
Midway Clark Printing, Wiltshire

Well wrapped up fisher lasses.

CONTENTS

ACKNOWLEDGEMENTS

The authors would like to offer thanks to:

North East Lincolnshire Museums Service, the *Grimsby Evening Telegraph,* and D.H. Armstrong for the use of their extensive photographic collections; Austin Mitchell MP for his valued support (and the transcribing machine!) Most importantly, thanks must go to all our workmates at the National Fishing Heritage Centre, not least Chris Hammond and Ged who were introduced, unwittingly, to the joys of transcription.

It is with great regret that we were unable to speak to Dolly Hardie who was involved in a car accident shortly before our interviews took place. Her struggle for fishermen's compensation is well documented in this book as elsewhere and epitomises the pivotal role of women in the deep sea fishing communities. We wish Dolly well, in both her recovery and campaign.

Alice Stizaker FLEETWOOD   Bernice Spriggs FLEETWOOD   Carol Spriggs FLEETWOOD   Dolly Waters GRIMSBY   Doreen Mersey FLEETWOOD   Edith Mewse GRIMSBY   Freda Whitelam GRIMSBY

Gwen Hallibone GRIMSBY   June Hewitt GRIMSBY   Kath Ferguson HULL   Lydia Sinclair GRIMSBY   Merle Boyington GRIMSBY   Molly Roberts GRIMSBY   Muriel Grant GRIMSBY

Muriel Greenbeck GRIMSBY   Muriel Waller GRIMSBY   Norma Griffiths GRIMSBY   Peggy Whittaker FLEETWOOD   Rita Stocks GRIMSBY   Trixie Godball GRIMSBY   Vera Hood HULL

The following is a list of those women interviewed during the compilation of this book. Without their honesty, patience, vivid, and often frank, recollections, this project would have been fruitless. We are extremely grateful to them all.

The initials of the appropriate contributor will appear at the foot of any extract taken from their interview unless otherwise stated:

Fleetwood
Jill Marr [JM]; Doreen Mersey [DM]; Alice Stizaker [AS]; Carol Spriggs and daughter [CS]; Peggy Whittaker [PW].

Grimsby
Merle Boyington [MB]; Trixie Godball [TB]; Muriel Grant [MG]; Muriel Greenbeck [MGb]; Norma Griffiths [NG]; Gwen Hallibone [GH]; Verda Jackson [VJ]; Edith Mewse [EM]; Molly Roberts [MR]; Lydia Sinclair [LS]; Rita Stocks [RS]; Muriel Waller [MW]; Doreen Waters [DW]; Freda Whitelam [FW].

Hull
Kath Ferguson [KF]; Olive Lazenby [OL]; Vera Hood [VH]; Vera Smith [VS]; and not forgetting Ron Ferguson [RF] – the sole male voice!

Milford Haven
Freda Woollard [FWo].

North Shields
Carol Bell [CB].

INTRODUCTION

The deep sea fishing community has often been portrayed, pilloried and parodied as an overtly masculine domain, home to the 'toughest job in the world' in which men 'worked hard and played hard'. However, women have, almost everywhere, been integral to the fishing community. Their onshore work has helped to build communities and their motherhood has shaped them.

Over one hundred hours of recollections and reminiscences have been recorded in Fleetwood, Grimsby, Hull, Milford Haven and North Shields in the first attempt of this kind to explore and define the lives and attitudes of women in these unique 'race apart' communities.

By discussing their position in relation to the home, workplace, community, and their beliefs and relationships, we hope to illustrate the significance of these women's cultural, social and economic role and the sacrifices they have made in playing it.

This book was originally conceived to support a new exhibition, 'The Role Of Women In Our Deep Sea Fishing Communities', at the National Fishing Heritage Centre. The book has, almost inevitably, acquired its own character – an amalgam of the tremendous depth, integrity, humility and good humour of its contributors. The guiding ethos of the exhibition, however, flows through the book. That is, that there are very few people more informed about an incident than those who have actually lived through it. This is their story, free from third party narrative.

We hope that this book will offer a resounding voice for the 'unsung heroines' of the fishing communities, providing chorus and verse to the assertion that they have tackled a history of harsh physical, psychological and economic barriers with great success.

Craig and Jenny Lazenby
1999

CHAPTER 1
Her story

Preparing fish for curing at Grimsby in the 1930s. Cured fish was sent from Grimsby to Southern Europe, South America, Cuba and the West Indies.

Roots

I came here [Grimsby] when I was seven. My father came fishing out of here and I came here with my brother and my sister. I'm the oldest. When we came here we was in rooms right 'til I was thirteen, you know we never had a house...we went to Albion Street, Orwell Street, Harlington Street. From there, he was fishing all the time and he got lost in the war, he went on convoy and he never came back no more. I was married young. I was married at sixteen to a fisherman and all, a chief engineer and he went to sea and then he got lost on the *Magnolia*, went down on the Humber and then I married another fisherman and that's where my story started you see.

EM

Political Roots

My father belonged to a very Conservative family, but when he came to Fleetwood, it was all poverty in Fleetwood in the '30s, he changed.

PW

Tough Roots

It's very difficult to remember the past because I don't have a big recollection of it. The only thing, the only thing I remember about my father is being constantly drunk and because of his drink my mother gave up and she'd lost interest in everything really, her family and everything. She was a mother at home, she never went out to work and she was always there for us but I think that she just had so much to cope with, with my father.

LS

Crew of the smack *City of Rome*, with families.

'Then there were boats by the thousand'. Grimsby fish dock, in 1901, during the lock-out.

Boom Town

She didn't know any other life but fishing 'cos her father before her was a fisherman, you see. That's what Grimsby people were. Fisher-folk. There was no other jobs – not to do. It was just continual fishing. Not like it is today. It's all gone and dwindled away. Then there was boats by the thousand in the dock.

MR

Family Tree

I was born here and there's five generations of my family live in his town. My father was a fisherman and his father had a small fleet of fishing boats sailing out of Ramsgate and going to Brixham. That was during the First World War when they were wooden boats and they all got blown up, no insurance so they didn't get anything for them. My father got his ticket in the '30s, went to Cardiff when the Depression was on and he walked it to

11

'Catch one, kiss one in a fish barrel'. Grimsby dock scene during the inter-war period.

Fleetwood met me mother and I was the first, I've just got a sister but my sister's married to a fisherman and then I married a fisherman and my father was a fisherman, skipper. You're not used to having men around the house, no men and then to top it all I had five girls so there's no men at all and five granddaughters!

PW

Play

At the top of the terrace you was all playing together and when it was the peace parties...and bonfire night they had the big bonfire in the middle of the street and the two shops. They would put a string across with Guy Fawkes on and let them go on the fire and such. I can still see my mam to this day. She got dressed up. It was one of the peace parties and she'd done this old bike up with red, white and blue which was crepe paper then like the streamers and she was riding that up and down the street and it had no tyres on. It was just the frame, you know, and me dad thought she was crazy for doing it.

KF

Kiss and Tell

We used to play in Riby Square...catch one kiss one, in a fish barrel, rounders. We all used to go over the lines, you know, where the railway line is 'cos it was all fish houses back there...until our parents said, 'C'mon, it's time you was all in.' I think it was happier times.

EM

Coronation Street

They had the street parties for the Coronation. It seemed to last forever. My mother made all the kids paper dresses and costumes, well all mothers did you know. But the community was there. Mothers could stand from one end – from one terraced house to another – and we'd play skipping. We were never left to our own devices. Do you know? Mother'd be in on the front playing with you. There was no chance for you to roam. The funniest thing – my brother was only a couple of years old and my mother put him on a clothes line to stop him from getting away from the terrace and all the neighbours used to watch him. They would go for a look at the bottom of the street, at me brother David. They watched each other's children and think nothing of drawing a hopscotch or ball games. They was allowed. They come out and pop the balls nowadays. Kids were in and out of each other's houses.

CS

Political Backstabbing

Well, when we was kids it was more Conservative...they used to vote for Wormersley. It was Strand Street School – it's still there – we used to have big sticks we used to put a poster on the top of these sticks and all stand outside, like a rivalry. We'd sing 'Vote, vote, vote for Mr Wormersley'. Then we'd say 'We'll stab 'em in the back' or something and we used to charge one another! Anyone would think it was worse than bloody grown-ups!

EM

Old Community

I will never forget this. He had got called out one night because they had bombed the Humber quite high and it was merchant ships and he went to unload this ship. It was a food ship but

'Vote, vote, vote for Mr Womersley'. Grimsby election poster, 1901.

The fish house: 'I think everyone was connected somewhere…you could not go anywhere without you smelled fish'.

the cases was damaged they was not supposed to do it so of course my dad did – corned beef and these tins of stew. You did not know what was in them – you knew the corned beef because of the shape of the tins but the rest you took pot luck what was in them. Word went round that the police was going to raid the houses, all the dockers' houses…so she said to me 'Come on, I want you to come to aunt Mag's with me'. Two suitcases full of this tinned stuff and that, for aunt Mag to hide. But aunt Mag wanted half of it…'I will have to have some of it because I would be in trouble for hiding it.' When she died it

was still there in that bedroom. Of course, she was the oldest sister, mum was the youngest and they was close and she had no teeth, only one in the front and it used to look massive to me and she called it her pickled onion stabber.

JH

Roll Out the Barrel

With the singing that was started on the night time, all the customers was regular on a Saturday and Sunday night, the favourite song was *Roll out the*

Barrel, you know. When I hear it on telly or the wireless now, it takes you back. You'll never be able to bring them days back.

MGb

Like it or Lump it

He [my father] was a docker and a lumper, if there was no work for the dockers they would send them lumping and you always knew – eleven o'clock for the twelve o'clock start you could hear the clogs clattering on the streets – used to wear clogs and there used to be a shop in Victoria Street called Shatfords. It used to sell nothing else but clogs, they used to be hung up outside in his window.

JH

Smell the Fish

I think nearly everybody had something to do with the fish industry. If they did not work direct on it; in a round about way, do you now what I mean? Because I mean now Riby Square end of Freeman Street where they have built them houses in Albert Place…was fish houses and the other was two-up, two-downs little cottages, you know. It did not matter where you went in the town there used to be, especially that end, something to do with the fishing industry – you could not go anywhere without you smelt the fish.

JH

George Shepherd, behind the bar of The Barrel, Freeman Street, Grimsby.

Lumping or 'bobbing' on the pontoon, Grimsby docks, in the 1930s.

Characters

With all these characters – they build up Hessle Road. Pam Stone...she was a giver in life. Most of Hessle Road fishermen would recognise straight away. She was a kind person, even though she was a card. She is one person I would like to be remembered. It's a pity no-one else has taken it up to her. The people that went to her funeral was unbelievable. The fishermen that turned up. Pigeon Smith...he came into a pub and asked if we wanted a chicken. It was in a carrier bag...when you held it, it weighed a ton – but it had a brick inside it. To make it feel as though it weighed more and it was just what he'd whipped off a stall. He was another character. Eva Smith – I mean she used to go in, they call it Round Oak – in station – but we always knew it as Tony Rice's from the original owner and she would say, 'Oh, buy us a drink' and somebody would say 'Well, show us your arse', sorry, and she would lift up her clothes and she never wore knickers!

KF

16

Give and Take

Pam, as I say, she even used to go to the Bethel and give there. These are things people wouldn't know about. She was one of life's givers and unfortunately, she seemed like she'd had life taken from her in the fact that she never seemed to have any good breaks.

KF

Boiled Alive!

You used to go onto the dock round Riby Square. Go round and all the blokes and the barrow boys used to whistle you. The dock was like a town on its own. You could buy anything from fish to sewing needles and cotton down there especially at Robinson's. He sold everything, clocks the lot, you could buy anything on the fish docks.

Me granddad James, because I think I was his little blue-eyed girl, one day he said 'Come on, cocker, come with me'. There was these lobsters because they are black lobsters before you cook them and they were alive and there was this big old copper and there wasn't one or two lobsters – he'd got loads. Where he'd got them from I don't know and he picked one up...I couldn't pick them up...and they were hissing as you put them in and he put the lid on it and waited five minutes for it to come out.

JH

Wake-up Call

They all used to like a good drink when they'd been at sea all that time. Big Eric, he was a Danish man. He used to have a good drink and then he used to lay his head on the table. Well,

Riby Square, Grimsby, *c.* 1950.

Left: Muriel Greenbeck at work in The Barrel, Grimsby. *Right:* Margo Robinson and Pam Stone. 'Pam – she is one person I would like to be remembered.'

they called his wife Mary, and she used to say, 'Muriel, will you go get me a cloth', and I used to get her this cloth and she used to lift his head off the table with his hair and slap his face with this dishcloth to wake him up.

MG*b*

Community Spirit

So they changed its name to Meadowell Estate but it's still The Ridges. I would say the majority of them [here] were from the fishing industry. I can remember you never locked your back door. You had a key hanging out the back o' your door, you know,

because our parents worked then, you know kids coming in from school. The community spirit was second to none. I think I was more frightened of my neighbours than my parents. You were never cheeky to your neighbours, it was always 'Mrs' this or 'auntie' this. I never called them by their first name and you'd never be cheeky to them because, in them days, neighbours would give them a clip around the lug as much as the parents did and there was this feeling of togetherness. It was like respect.

CB

CHAPTER 2
Beliefs

Muriel Grant launches the *Dennis Hall*.

Keeping Faith

We went to Sunday school and everything when I was a girl. But when my children were born I gave them the option, I never drummed it in them that they had to go. If they wanted to go to Sunday school they could go but if they didn't want to it was up to them but, you see, I still believe in God. I say my prayers every night I go to bed. How many women do that? But, I still do. When my grandchildren used to sleep with me and I'd say my prayers they used to say, 'Have you heard Nana saying her prayers?' I've never missed – all me life.

MG

Once a Catholic…

She was a Catholic and my father wasn't. He wasn't religious but he didn't like her going to Catholic church. And, I can remember, she'd go to Catholic church while he was away and Fisher en's Bethel while he was home.

VS

Miura Mystery

The story of the discovery of my father's body. She went, *Miura*, she foundered on the rocks at Stanbury Mouth which is in north Cornwall. It was a dreadful night and there were seven saved and five lost, one of which was my father. My grandmother never ever would believe or accept the fact that her son was dead and she, over a period of months, constantly had what the local parish priest said were visions and she dreamt these very vivid dreams of my father's body laying on a sandy beach with his head on his arm. My grandfather was the local school attendance officer in Milford and went to the local parish priest and asked him if he would write to the incumbent of the parish wherein Stanley Mouth is. And the incumbent wrote back, and I have all the papers to say he would have a watch put on this particular little bay and in the August after the *Miura* foundered, they interrupted Evensong to say there was a body had been left at the high water mark and it was lying face down in the sand with its face on its arm. Now these men didn't know of my grandmothers dream but it was exactly as she'd dreamed it and the body was removed from the beach and put in a little beach hut where a lady used to serve teas in the summer. Now, bear in mind that this was in 1927. And there was an inquest held and because of the length of time that the body had been in the water it was not recognisable as my father but it was too much of a coincidence to dismiss it out of hand – that it could have been another body...and he is buried in that little churchyard beside a grey Cornish granite memorial which is a memorial to all unknown seamen washed up constantly on that beach. My mother was never able to afford to go back again, and in 1960 I took my mother back and all around this lonely boat house were photographs of wrecks that had been on that particular stretch of coast...and low and behold there was *Miura* and this boatman remembers going to the site of the wrecks and clambering down over it and his words to me were, 'Oh, I was up to me waist in fish, lovely it was'. That's exactly what that Cornishman said to me and told us that *Miura*'s ship bell was a dinner gong in one of the hotels in Bude.

FWo

The Spirits

She used to go to Spirits. She used to love going to the Spirits, even though she was Catholic. She'd go to a place on the Boulevard and she sometimes used to take us but she didn't get dressed up to go. Me dad didn't like that – going to the Spirits – so we never told him. I used to think it was really interesting. We used to have a fortune teller called Mucky Violet and she used to read cards – she was brilliant, I used to love to go. My mum used to walk round and pick her up and come back and then she always packed her up – tea, sugar, butter – she always used to have a bag of something to give Mucky Violet. A lovely woman, she was. She would come and read your cards or read your tea cup and she used to say she loved coming to Beattie's, because she never had any money, Mucky Violet. And me mother used to get her ten Woodbines.

VS

Fisherman's chapel, Central Hall, Grimsby.

Deathless Days

I can honestly say that my life as a child was bounded by, I suppose one would call it, the cold hand of Welsh Non-Conformism, bounded by school and chapel full stop. I mean chapel three times a day, no messing. I view my Sundays as a child as deathless days, not now. I don't know when I came to the age of reason, but I accepted it and I went.

FWo

Paying Respects

We had to go to Fishermen's Bethel, we had to go to Sunday school. If there were services for people lost at sea, we had to go to that but, he never actually went. It was respect, wasn't it? For people lost at sea. I think my mum would have liked us to be Catholics, but she never mentioned that when my dad was home from sea.

VS

Churched

That was the done thing, if you like. I mean, it was like when you had your children, you used to go to church as soon as you came out the home. I had two of mine at home – two of my eldest. Or soon as you get out of bed you're booked to see the vicar to get churched 'cos you couldn't go in anyone's house until you was, 'cos it was supposed to be unlucky. People like my mum, you know – their generation – you wouldn't get over the doorstep if you weren't churched.

MR

Father vs Father

I can remember the priest coming once and saying – well, not saying – we were bastards. But she was a Catholic and he was non-Catholic and they'd been married in the Bethel – that we weren't legitimate. And me dad threw him out. And I can remember as plain as day that he was annoyed to think that the priest was suggesting that my mother was living in sin and he'd produced seven illegitimate children. And he was absolutely bloody furious about that. But my mother was, in a funny way, upset 'cos he'd thrown the priest out. But, she'd go to the Catholic church and take us – the little ones, not the older ones.

VS

Superstition

I wanted to go to sea with my father and I used to say, 'Are you taking me to sea, dad?' and I got on his nerves that much that he said to mum 'Well, pack her some clothes together and I'll take her'. We were walking down Orwell Street and I said to my dad, 'Will we get lost at sea?' 'You're not coming no more', he said. 'When we go out there, we don't think about getting lost'. So he made me go home.

EM

Coloured Outlook

Oh gosh no! Washing your husband away and all that lot? Ron was [superstitious], Ron was dreadful. I spent ages knitting him a beautiful sweater, it was like a lovely green and he went to sea in it one trip. Anyway, the next time I put it in his stuff…because his mother used to knit his sea jerseys…it was on the bed. If Ron went to sea and made a bad trip, whatever he was wearing caused it.

PW

'Wiggies'

Specially, like if you was a fisherman's wife. You never washed the day he went away. You didn't use the word P I G. We still don't. It's just…we always say 'wiggy' – we do to the grandkids an' all. My little two year old – he calls them wiggies…but that's Roy. You know – if we've got anybody here – 'cos there's a lot of people use that word…I can see his face. He cringes, he does. It's like – you didn't wash the day they went away 'cos they used to say you was washing them away. You didn't say the word P I G. Most fishermen didn't like green. They thought it was an unlucky colour. Just how different people was with the superstitions. You know, I always would wait two days till I knew Roy was out the dock – and then I used to wash. Isn't it funny how communities have altered from then till now?

MR

St Romanus

One trawler – I think it was the *Romanus* – it set sail three times and came back and me dad said, 'Off it, sign off it'. He got sacked. They had all those superstitions and I said to me mum, 'If he signs off what's gonna happen?' And me mum said 'Your dad's right. He should not sail on that'. And I think it went down. [*St Romanus*]

VS

Guilty Conscience

You could always go meet them in dock but you could never see them go out. You did stick to it because if you did not you would feel the consequences if you washed on the day. If they went to sea and something happened you would feel that you had washed them out to sea.

RS

Seeing

I was always awake waiting for the key to come in that door. Before he died I seemed to get a premonition. I said to one of my sisters about it. I said, 'Me husband Tom's come home with his black suit on'. I said, 'He's been into the bedroom to children'. One of me daughters said, 'Yeah, he lifted me bed up, mum'. I said, 'Did he? He'd been to see that you were alright'. Then, you see, he died shortly after. That must have been my warning.

DM

Left: 'Off it, sign off it'. Vera Smith's father, Fred Young. *Right:* Olive Lazenby as a young girl, Hessle Road, Hull.

All Washed Up

She followed all the superstitions. I don't know why really. Maybe she believed them, maybe she didn't know any different. I don't know…But, you see I'm like that now because if Graham goes away I won't wash. Even if my daughter goes away, I will not wash and I will not strip a bed and I won't go and see them off. So, you see, it's inbred, isn't it?

VS

Portents

My eldest brother…he picked up this mine in the net and it exploded. I think the skipper was killed – I don't know about the mate…he lost everything that trip. It wasn't funny really but that day – me mother had a budgie and she used to let it fly around the living room and she had a bowl of water – I think she was washing windows or something and the budgie fell in this bowl of water and me mum said, 'Oh, I don't like that'. That day she got to know my brother's ship went down.

OL

CHAPTER 3
Home

A baby outside a terraced house in New
Street, Grimsby, in the 1920s.

Bearers

Don't forget then, there wasn't your birth control or anything like that and don't forget, then you could say no and they could still have their way with you. So, therefore all these with big families. That was their right to give it and that's where a lot of it would be. They thought that was their right – to use that woman however they wanted to and they did – 'cos that was their chattel. You had to be very strong or [have] an understanding husband that thought of you not as a chattel but as a partner and I do think a lot of it was naivety.

KF

Alice Stizaker in 1956. This was shortly after the birth of her second son.

Loss

I had a sister that died when she was seven hours old and me dad was going to sea and I know me mum was in labour and he didn't really want to go, and they said, 'Look Dave, if you don't go, you've missed a ship'. Anyway, me mum lost the baby. She was a blue baby. It died. Dad never saw it. Never saw the funeral or anything 'cos he had to go to sea else he'd have been in jail. I mean they wouldn't have done that to a man working ashore.

CS

Seasick

When I was pregnant with her [our daughter] he carried her. I wasn't sick, he was. I said, 'Why didn't you do it for all the other three as well?' They all said, 'What's the matter with you? You're sick' and I hadn't been a bit sick. I said, 'Well, you're having my morning sickness. That makes a change'.

DM

Enough is Enough

He would have had more but I put the damper on him and went and had the operation. He would have had more, yes but I says, 'No. I've had enough. I can't cope anymore'. There comes a time in your life when you've done your share. I mean, four children, you just can't carry on like that.

DM

Molly Roberts and daughter. 'They missed all the growing up.'

King Dick

I went to watch him in and I was stood on the Lock pits. He came off. He had the original sea bag and he come round the corner and he said, 'What was the fist for?' I said, 'I'm pregnant'. He said, 'You can't be!' I said, 'I am and I've told Dr Richardson that I'm gonna string you up from the Yard Arm on the Mount'. He thought he was King Dick. We had the biggest and best pram in Fleetwood!

AS

Growing Pains

Like for instance, one trip they was born when they came in, wasn't they? Then they came in three months after. They was feeding on solids and then they was crawling and they missed all the in-

between things, you know, with the kids. I think it really is a shame and I think this is why a lot of these fishermen dote on their grandchildren – 'cos they do. I've known Ray dote on the grandkids…it's as I say, because they missed all the growing up. 'Me wife's had a baby'. And that was it. Like I say, one trip they was doing this, one trip they was doing something else. All the teething – I wasn't saying they were in bed all night, 'cos they wasn't – but, they wasn't up all night with the bairn and two or three others and you still had to get up the next day and sort things out.

MR

Magnificent Seven

I once said to her, 'Why did you have so many kids?' I think that she had

27

Children on a boat, Grimsby, in the 1950s.

more than seven, but seven survived. She said there was no way not to have seven 'cos in those days there wasn't the contraceptive. I don't really think she regretted the seven kids...I think that, like a lot of other women of that generation, she would have left if she had somewhere to go that would take seven kids.

VS

Mother and Father

He was constantly drunk. My father's favourite expression, all our lives, was 'Children should be seen and not heard'. So you learned from a very early age that you stayed out of his way. When he was slightly drunk, he was always in a good mood and he used to say 'Here's a pound' or whatever but he never showed any interest in us

whatsoever, he never ever took us out, never came to anything to do with school and this had the knock on effect with mother...I think she was just ground down, so ground down. That's the other thing with my father. You never ever brought your friends home when he was home.

LS

One-parent Family

I just took the ten to two shift, like. But I didn't go to work when he was fishing. I stayed at home. 'Cos the kids can't do without both of you, can they really? Not at the end of the day. It wasn't bad.

MR

The Good Life

We would take a milk bottle back, because you got a penny on a milk bottle when you took it back, to go swimming. We really had a good life when we was kids as me mum did what I did and many others. They spent their money when they had any spare, remembering that it was coupons then, they spent that on you and they came second.

KF

Unforgiven

I think going to sea with the trawlers, which I'm sure looking back now he didn't want to do, but he had to earn a living, he resented it and he resented us and he used to say how much we'd ruined his life but he never ever saw the drink. It's a hard life at sea, I mean I know about it, he hated it. I'm sure he did but I can't ever and will never ever forgive my father. I don't think he knew what being a father meant.

LS

Change for the Better?

I don't know how happily married she was but I know she often – when she was getting older and going on change – would say she would have liked a different life but who would take her on with seven kids? And when I look back it was just work for her. And what can you do with seven kids and your husband's gone to sea and is away for three weeks? So, she was totally responsible and didn't do a bad job, I don't think.

VS

Rearing

I think it was your temperament. It was either your children being brought up properly or going on the streets, wasn't it? So I made my way by saying I'd bring my children up and I've got three children that I'm very proud of. I got one that's a captain and one that's a mate and I got a girl that's very, very ladylike. Been brought up like a lady.

A child fetches some water, off Freeman Street, Grimsby in the 1920s.

VIEWPOINT VIEWPOINT

My fisherman daddy

SIR,—My Daddy is a fisherman. He is not a drunk and I do not wait in pub doorways for him.

He is a good, kind daddy who loves me very much and works very hard for me.

I think the people who wrote those nasty things about fishermen are horrid.

Lots of my Daddy's friends let me call them Aunty and Uncle.

Lots of my "uncles" are fishermen, and they are good and kind, too.— LORNA DENNESS, aged 7½, Horsegate Road, Goxhill.

The other side of the story, *Grimsby Evening Telegraph*, 26 July 1975.

Very happy. So, I've got nothing to complain about. So, as I say, it's not been an easy life and I wouldn't recommend it to anybody. No.

MG

Drunk as a Skunk

The thing I resent most – more than anything – is that none of us reached our potential. You were never encouraged, you were never supported. Maybe it's nothing to do with my father being at sea, maybe it's the type of person that he was. But I'd had from nine to sixteen with him being a fisherman. Well, nine to seventeen because it was about a year after Johnny died that he gave up the sea. I was a brilliant athlete at school and won every race…and neither of my parents ever came to watch me. Except once when my father came so you can imagine how pleased I was and then how disappointed I was when he was falling all down, drunk as a skunk. I was so embarrassed. He came up to me and his arm was round you and then this awful slurry voice…and he's saying drunkenly how proud he is of you but then never remembering the next day and never mentioning it again.

LS

Good as Gold

Oh, I'll tell you a story about my eldest one. She was about a couple or three months old – and we lived with me mum then. She was as good as gold while he was away – and every time he was in dock she used to scream and scream at night. I bet you he used to just get in bed and she used to start and she used to look at him – as little as she was – she used to look at him as if to say, 'Who are you?', and most of the night he used to spend walking up and down the bedroom with her. Anyway, me mam said, 'You can't have this all the while he's in dock'. The first night he went away she was as good as gold. That was because I was in there with her, on her own, and as little as she was, she knew. We used to move the cot in with me mum while he was in dock and as she got older she gradually took to him, like. But she was the only one of mine that did that…I used to say, 'I can't believe her – she's as good as gold'.

MR

Happy Christmas

Christmas used to come around and we all used to buy Christmas presents and I suppose this was the worst. Until I grew up and I left home I can't ever, and I mean this, ever remember having a happy Christmas. Christmas was a nightmare in our house…if it was at all possible he was never at sea at New Year. The build up to Christmas time, like for any child was always exciting…and then Christmas day used to come and my mother made a small effort but not a big effort. We never got a lot of Christmas presents we might only get one or two. Christmas morning used to come, the pubs opened at eleven, my father used to go to the pub at eleven, they closed at one. He used to be at home by 1.30 and so drunk that he couldn't eat his Christmas dinner. So we're sitting there waiting to eat a Christmas dinner and there's been no participation in preparing the meal, getting the meal ready by the family…and you just know that it's going to be another awful day. So

St Mary's Roman Catholic primary school, Heneage Road, Grimsby, 1950s.

Christmas day used to be like any other day – you used to think how are you going to stay out of his way…and of course the period at home was short again over Christmas and New Year period. It was a relief when he went away…on everybody's part because you weren't having to contend with the drink and you weren't having to curtail your personality. You weren't having to think what you could say and what you could do.

LS

Convenience Foods

My dad wouldn't have dreamed of going shopping. I mean, a couple

'His kids and wife came first in a peculiar way'. Vera Smith's father, Fred Young.

of days in dock, he wouldn't go shopping. Me mother used to go to Riby Square to meet him…I can honestly say, when my dad used to come in there was a cooked dinner ready for him. Even when she used to go and meet him, there was a cooked dinner ready for him.

VJ

Downtown

If he was in from sea, him and me mam and the family used to go down town…used to get a quarter of sweets. Me mam used to get a box of limes, you know? Chocolate limes and then we used to get a bag of fruit and from there back up the tram track and back home.

LD

In at the Deep End

He treated them [when he was home] and he always used to take them down to office. And I always remember, he was gonna learn them to swim and I thought he was taking them to the bath but he took them to sea wall and threw them in the water. But he said 'They'll learn, like I learned'. And they're all good swimmers!

AS

Hit 'em First

I suppose when I was younger I never knew of the hard life the fishermen were having at sea. I just knew that dad used to go and come home with this great big sea bag and we used to see what he'd brought us. We were tough. I was tough. 'Hit 'em first and ask questions later', me dad used to say. I don't do that now! I think that when me dad landed and had had a good trip, we were millionaires. I'm sure that's how we thought. We were always looked after. We never went without for me dad and mum to go out. His kids and wife came first in a peculiar sort of way. He was very strict. We did come first and I don't know how other fishermen were with the wives.

VS

Can't Buy Love

I think some of them [fishermen] think that money buys everything. They get it into their heads. But it doesn't. It doesn't buy love. I mean, this is what I tried to explain to him. You should get hold of your children and love them. But he wasn't that type of a person. I said, 'Money doesn't buy it. You can buy them all of the sweets and give 'em money, but it doesn't buy the love'.

DM

Husband and Father

He was a good dad – I mean, I thought the world of him but I wouldn't have said he was a good husband. I used to look forward to him coming home but I was always with me mum. I think I looked forward to me bar of chocolate.

OL

Hi-de-Hi

From being born to being sixteen we were actually taken away on holiday once and I'll never forget it. From being born to being twenty, [it] was the best day of my life. Because they took us to Butlin's in its hey day but I can honestly say from nine to six we never saw them and maybe that's why it was the best week of our lives. My twin brother and I we used to go to them and ask them for sixpence, if we found them, during the day and that's as much contact as we had with them for the whole week. So I don't know how they performed that week…and there was a talent competition and I went in that and I won that and neither of them knew about it.

LS

A Mother's Place

When I got married, my husband decided that…he was old fashioned in that respect, that if children arose – which they did quite quickly – there would be no chance of me working. A mother's place is in the home, especially with a man that goes to sea, because they'd need one parent on hand.

CS

Northern Sun

I believe he was on the *Northern Sun*, the first trip out…the ship had to be refitted out and checked and that, like they do a new boat. He thought he'd go and have a trip in the North Sea while

33

he was waiting and that's when he got dragged in with the wynch, through a Deckie learner. When he first came home [after the accident] my youngest sister, she screamed. She said, 'No, no. My own daddy. I want my own daddy'. She wanted her own daddy, not that daddy 'cos he was all scarred and cut. He came home looking like a mummy. I know I was thirteen. I was young but I can see him as if it was today.

NG

Goody Bag

Our dad, he went to sea and he died when I was seven but I can always remember him coming up dock 'cos he used to bring a load of crabs in the bottom of his bag and a bit of scented soap. There was this lovely tablet there and you were frightened to take the wrapper off and spoil it. He used to make his cakes nearly as big as the plate and he used to make brawn, toffee and all sorts 'cos he used to be the ship's cook.

DW

Three-day Millionaires

When they had a good trip there wasn't anybody that did not know because it came straight off the dock. When Harold came home you always knew. As I had just come home from work and there would be bags all over the floor, he had been to spend his earnings – his settlings – on his family. They had been in the town shopping and they had called in at my mothers and there would be bags all over the

'Down dock.' Grimsby no. 2 dock, 1969.

34

The ship's cook. 'Cakes nearly as big as the plate'.

floor. If there was anything the bairns wanted, he made sure that they got it.

VH

Good Father

Ron for instance – personally, he was a good father to the kids. They didn't want for a thing.

KF

Hot Cakes

My father used to – we'd go to bed at night and he'd come in early morning. He used to shout us. He'd stand at the bottom of the stairs and he used to shout, 'Come on, you lazy lot. Get out of bed and come and see what I've got for you'. And you could smell 'em. Hot cakes. You'd go down and they were coming out the oven, red hot and lashes of butter on for you – before you went to school. And then they would buy a pig. We had a small holding at the back. They'd geese and they'd chickens. She looked after everybody. She never had gone out to work in her life, you see. Her mother died when she was sixteen and her sister died when she was sixteen and they left seven kids. So we ended up with twenty-two people living in one house on Corporation Road. We used to be seven of us in a bed.

MG

Night Shift

I wasn't there to take her to school, I wasn't there to pick her up. I used to work half past seven 'til half past four, so I had to rely on other people. Anyhow, one day one of the charge hands said to me 'You want a night shift?' I said, 'Yeah, 'cos I've got a little girl who's only six and her dad died and I'm not there to take her to school. I've got to get a neighbour. I'm not there to pick her up from school'. He went away and come back and said, 'Friday night you start your night shift' and I went on nights there and I've been on nights for twenty years. I was in my twenty-first year but I didn't complete it, because I retired. I did night hygiene, cleaning machines, pressure guns and everything.

NG

Around the Table

They loved their dad. When he came home we would sit around the table there and get the wine out and have a proper meal, a dinner.

PW

Night shift. Ross group fish processing plant, 1956.

Landing Day

When he was in dock he used to go out with them on the landing day and that was the only day he got with them really. He used to have a day out with his mates and we would have the landing day out and it was more or less time for him to go back to sea. Two nights in dock a bit of time with the kids. If it was a weekend they got a bit longer – come in Thursday night, land Friday and have Saturday and Sunday and then go away Monday morning. The kids used to love it. Yes, because he had a tin of goodies and a few bars of soap, but of course as they got older they got a handful so he give fishing up. He want to sea for about twenty year I should say.

RS

Strict but Kind

They were very, very kind. Strict but kind. They always liked us to be nice and warm at night, you know. Every morning you got a cup of tea with a spoon of brandy in it to start the day. His parents must have done the same.

VS

His Father's Son

If owt went wrong, he used to pick on lad. I'd say, 'Eh, leave him alone. You were a little boy once'. They didn't have a lot of patience when they came home, fishermen.

DM

'They were very, very strict but kind.' Vera Smith and twin sister, Anne.

Minding the Kids

I wouldn't say a lot of them went to work – them with children couldn't really, could they. My mother-in-law, she married a fisherman and he was a fisherman all his life. She had – ten, twelve children. So, I mean, she couldn't go to work. I mean, no-one's gonna mind ten kids, are they?

GH

Home from School

I think he would probably think that he wasn't being a very good husband if she had to work to support us. She had

Skipper Kelly on GY531 Harrowby.

Table Manners

I think it's drilled in you. My mother was Victorian type, if you can understand. Her word was law in the house. You see, he was away at sea – my father and uncle. There was only mother there so her word was law in the house. When we were sat at the table, we were not allowed to leave it till everybody was finished and not allowed to speak at the table When she had company – when she entertained – and we were in the room we had to sit very quiet. We weren't allowed to interrupt. We weren't allowed to say a word. If you did she was up. She was that kind of person.

MG

Discipline

Well if my oldest brother was here he'd tell you. She used to sit with a cane on the table – a lot of people, well, most houses used to, you know. She was mother and father.

MR

Mother's the Ogre

Roy would never tell them off while he was home because he used to say, 'It's not fair 'cos I'm only there two days out of a month'. In a way it was right. It's like all the world over, isn't it? The mother's always the ogre. I doesn't matter what state, the mother is always the ogre. My kids say now, 'Me dad never used to shout at

to be there when we went to school and there when we came home from school and she was. The first thing you said when you came through the door was, 'mum'.

VS

Torn

Oh, I think it was harder for the men 'cos we were left with the children. We were left with part of them on a day to day basis. Left with part of them to bring up and you saw things in the children.

CS

38

me. Me dad never used to say I couldn't do anything'. Well, there you go. Mother's always the ogre. You know how you see Roy, don't you? Well, that's the way he mainly is. And I've got three daughters and a son and, as me and you are sat here now, I could bawl and shout my head off and they just wouldn't take a blind bit of notice they used to give me all this back. Our Roy could be sat like this, just talking to them – telling them off – but only as we're talking and the tears used to be streaming down my daughters' faces and I used to watch and think 'I don't believe that'. And now, as old as they all are now, they don't like him to say anything. Now if I say anything they turn round and…but they always have something to say to me. But if he says anything they walk away and I still seen him – as old as they are now – bring tears to their eyes. Isn't it funny? And he's not an aggressive man, He just – I don't know – it's just how he is.

MR

When the Cat's Away

When he was there they did not need discipline, it was just when he was not there…

That was one of the things while they were at sea you had to be mother and father to them.

RS

Who's the Boss?

I don't remember ever being hit by my dad. I remember being hit by my mum, you know, but not very often. My dad, what he said, that was it.

VS

Whack!

Their favourite was – you'd hide and off course you got under the table, 'Come on out and I won't touch you'. 'Oh, yes you will'. 'I won't'. You'd get from under the table. Whack! You felt your head go into next week! But you

A child poses for the camera off Freeman Street, Grimsby in the 1920s.

39

knew she was the boss. That was me mum. We seldom did anything wrong 'cos we knew she was the boss.

CS

Home Sweet Home

They come home, they'd break homes up, they'd give you a black eye for it. Call you all the filthy names under the sun and you never did anything. What could you do with three children? You were home looking after them.

MG

Double Whammy

It was a hard life for both mother and father. But what I used to love about it, though – they had very long memories. If you did anything wrong – mother was the boss while dad was away – but when dad came home, dad knew as well. Yes, so you got disciplined twice. Whether it was a deterrent to say, 'You won't do it again – you'll get two lots of discipline', I'm not sure.

CS

Hell's Bells

You had to be mother and father to your children…I didn't knock hell's bells out of them but they were chastised because I didn't believe in waiting for him coming in from sea and saying, 'They've done that and they've

done that'. I couldn't see the point of that, so I did it.

LD

Keeping Quiet

When he was in drink he really used to hit us and I don't mean a smack, I mean a belt and not with a belt, but properly with a fist and we were marked and we were bruised and there was never any remorse. We didn't think it was the norm it was just that you actually stayed out of his way, you kept very quiet and it's very hard for people of today, or children of today to understand that you never sat in his seat. If you were sat in his seat, it was never 'Oh, I want to sit down', it was a clip round the ear 'ole. It was always aggressive. He just wasn't a happy man. He didn't beat us for no reason, we were always naughty…I just mean the normal things that a child does and you would be hit and you would be hit hard.

LS

Code of Conduct

He has never ever laid a finger on any of ours. No, I don't think they did. No, you was their mother and father and you was the one that had to give them a code of conduct. Having said that, only once did Ron ever touch my oldest daughter. She wasn't a bad girl actually, being the first she had everything, you know. But it was when she was coming up to getting married and she was lippy to me and he clipped

40

Muriel Waller and friend, aged sixteen.

Vera Smith's brothers and sister.

her on the ear.

KF

Friendly Warning

He used to leave [the discipline] to me mam, you know, 'cos he used to say, 'If I hit youse, you're killed'…that was enough!

LD

Policeman's Advice

I got home and I daren't go in the house. I knew I was going to get a good hiding. I daren't go in. Anyway, I was walking the streets – this is the God's honest truth – this policeman got hold of me, said, 'What you think you're doing?' I said, 'I daren't go home'. He said, 'why?' I said, 'Cos I'm late going home and I'll get a good hiding'. He said, 'Who off?' I said, 'Me dad'. He said, 'Well you know you got to face your dad in the morning so you may as well get a good hiding tonight as in the morning'. Anyway he took me home. I didn't get a good hiding that night – but I did the next day. I didn't stop out late no more!

MW

Moon on a Stick

She was very strict [mother]. If the lads did anything wrong she'd march them round to the police station. She never waited 'til my dad came home. We never got 'Wait 'til your father gets home', which I thought was quite strong for a lady, you know. If there was a problem or we needed discipline she did it there and then. He was a strict disciplinarian. We took notice. You didn't argue with me dad. You didn't argue with me mother, come to that. Apart from the fact that he was home and the moon was yours if you wanted it.

VS

CHAPTER 4

Empowerment or emburdenment

Merle Boyington shows neighbours how to braid in the back yard.

A Hard Life

My mum – she was…how can I explain it? She was a good woman and she never wasted money. Whenever they came in with their money and their settlings…some of it was put in a bank and some was put to buy a house. And she really did work hard herself but never went out to work – but she worked hard in the home. She used to do the knitting for them. The Hob socks and all the black and white jerseys. She knitted for me when I was a little lass. She knitted all my clothes and everything. How can I explain it? The wages wasn't very good at all. Poor. Very poor wages. They only made big money if they had the fish to market and if it sold and they got a lot of money that was wonderful. My father gave my mother it, you see, so she used to bank it. I think that Pat was three months and although my mother then had money it didn't make her any different – she was still poor. She said to me, 'You'll have to get a job part time'. So I went braiding, making fisher nets. I did it in Sixhills Street. I could only do it part time – mornings and before I could go to work I had to get up and get my mother's breakfast and the baby ready, feed the baby and that. Then I used to braid 'til dinner time. When I come home at dinner, she'd done no work in the house, had mother. She'd cleaned the baby and done the food – but then I'd have to start doing house work. Then at night – I'd brought work home with me nets to make me wages up. I stood in the garage with a pole across braiding till three or four in the morning, in the bitter cold, with a scarf around me neck to keep me warm. So, it's been a very hard life. Now, you can't believe that, but it's the gospel truth. Aye, it's been a hard life.

MG

Whose Bill?

He didn't know what it was to pay a bill really. I mean when he settled, he'd come up and he'd say what he took and then he gave me so much money and he'd keep a bit for himself and I would have the running of the house and pay all the bills.

EM

Edith Mewse outside her Grimsby home in the 1960s.

Settling Down

We are Hessle Road born and bred and we now live in the high rise flats at Great Thornton Street. When our husbands went to sea, the major things was making your money spread out or going down the dock for your money. As you did not get it sent home you had to go down dock and get it. Settling would help you through the time they were at home and to get your extras such as your bairns clothing or paying the odd bill or such. There is one thing I would say, it was very rare that Ron ever came home to a bill because I paid them before he came home, but making your money spin was very hard, you know when you have children to support. As I was saying, down Hessle Road we had the Clothing House, one was the ladies and one for the men and from there when you did your settling on the dock you went into Rayners.

KF

Financial Restraint

My mother used to always go down to meet him when he was being paid just to make sure she got her money because if she didn't he'd spend it. Of course, then they got their bonuses and everything, if you didn't catch him before the pubs opened because he gambled as well, a lot. He would lose every penny in the three or four days he was home. I always remember him saying, 'Oh, you take everything I've got. You've got all my money'. But it was only his wages and all the time he was at sea, mum had to feed, clothe us, pay the bills and she was the person who did pay the bills. My father never had the money to pay anything. Everything in the house was organized by my mother and had it not been for her – and she'd got a little bit of money of her own from her first marriage – we would have been on the streets because he could never have kept a home together, he could never have paid a mortgage because every penny he had went on drink and gambling.

LS

Share System

I used to get me wages and landing day when we used to go out and meet all the crew and what-have-you. We used to go shopping. If the kids wanted shoes or anything we used to get them that and what was left, he used to share with me. So. It was good, yes.

MR

Live for Today

The money that was brought into your house. Had that man been more responsible instead of 'live for today', you'd have had a bank book as long as your arm. I mean, you did get some good blokes but a lot of them just frittered their money away, you know. The one thing we never argued about was money if it was there, it was there. If it wasn't, it wasn't.

KF

Good Saver

Roy's always been a good saver. Say he had two shillings, he could save half of that and if he had a trip off he always had enough to cover my wages. I never went without a week's wages. Whereas, a lot of them, if they had a trip off, they had a trip off and it was hard luck, do you know what I mean? But he was never like that. If he had three weeks off, I used to get my three week's wages. He was good in that respect, Roy.

MR

Money Down the Drain

I mean the pubs down here made a lot of money out of fishermen. 'Cos that's where the money went. The women didn't get it. You were very lucky if you got a load of money. Some of the skipper's wives – and mates did, but not many I don't think. No, no. And if they don't have the fish, didn't catch the fish and it wasn't a good market, didn't have money to come home to. More often as not, they could land in debt. Or they would sup the money before they went to sea so when they came back they was still in debt. So, how could they give you money if they hadn't got it?

MG

Throwing it Away

Me dad'd walk up the street when we was kids and he'd say to himself, 'Oh there's change in me pocket'. Coins, half-crowns and God knows what. He'd throw it to the kids on the street and me mother'd say to herself 'It's nearly as much as a week's wages he's throwing away to the kids'.

CS

A Fighter

Very strong willed as you've gathered. A fighter. I was determined that I wouldn't go under, 'cos when my mother got to know that I'd got on with him, she didn't like it at all. And I would never let her say that I couldn't manage. Never let her rub it in. 'She'll be back', she used to say, 'she'll come back. She'll never stick it'. Oh, determined. You've only got to say that to me, dear. It's like the jobs. They said, how can you do three jobs. I said, 'I'll keep my children'. They had everything they wanted. Well kept, well fed, well clothed. Best of everything I could provide for them. I never asked for a penny anywhere.

MG

Jobless

He came home one day and we knew the Icelandic fishing grounds were closing and the firm kept the home waters ships going for a short while and they couldn't carry on because they relied on the Icelandic business. So he went in the office one afternoon and they said 'Sorry, Ron the firm's closing down'. Ron came home and just said, 'I'm out of work'. You know, I mean it just hit you…he was very fretful and

Muriel Waller (second from the left), with family and friends.

very restless. Very, very difficult because you'd no income. I wanted to go for quarantine kennel and he wanted to go for the boat and I thought well, he's worked for what we've got. It was the biggest mistake of our lives because we ended up losing the house. We had our home repossessed because Ron wasn't an inshore fisherman, he hadn't a clue and he was trying to run the boat, trying to do everything and it was no good. He was deep water, he was used to big trips, big fish and not scratting around the Cumbrian coast. It was a terrible mistake.

PW

On the Horses

One time I come in and he said, 'I've lost the mortgage money'. I said, 'What? You didn't'. He said 'I lost the mortgage money'. I said, 'I know where you lost that. On horses'. I said, 'You can't kid me, you know'. But what a struggle to get that mortgage back. I had to pay all the bills. I had to see to everything. At the end of the day, that's why I got a little job. So that the kids didn't go short of food.

DM

Settle in Debt

Yes, well I remember my sister. I mean her husband was a fisherman – and they often used to settle in debt, you know because they had not got the amount of fish and so if they settled in debt they had no money, so they would come and borrow off the family.

VH

House Hunting

I think when you're married to fishermen you tend to become a bit bossy – you're your own woman, you do

Vera Smith's father, Fred Young is pictured at age fourteen, before his first trip.

everything yourself. I can remember his mother saying to me, 'Buy a house and you need a mortgage'. There's me going to the counter and looking over the counter at these people and saying 'I want to buy a house and they don't think that somebody at nineteen can go in and tell them they want to buy a house – not them days. Ron earned enough money to be able to put £500 in a house that cost £2,500 which is a lot when you can do that.

PW

A Good Manager

I mean, mum used to get her housekeeping every week which never seemed to be enough but she was always a good manager…she wasn't allowed to get into any debt, he wouldn't have any debt, so she didn't and I often wondered how she did it. But she used to knit jumpers and things for the Scotch wool shop on Hessle Road and she used to get paid sixpence an ounce which helped to make ends meet, I suppose.

VS

Dress for Parish

Well, if they were going back that was okay and you could get a sub on your wages but if they weren't you had to go to what they called parish then. You know, to give you something to tide you over while they got back in a ship and such as. It was really hard. The funny thing was, in them days, if you had to go to what was called parish you couldn't go tidy. If you went tidy, you looked as though you had too much so you didn't get anything anyway.

KF

We'll be All Right

When I had Roy and he was four or five we started going on day trips. Used to go out on coach trips. I used to love that. It took all them years to get a bit of money in the bank and he was in one of the top ships and he came in and he said, 'We're settling for six weeks', he said, 'I'll sign on the dole. We'll be all right, won't we?' After the six weeks they told him at the office she'd been sold to Lowestoft as a stand-by boat.

AS

Turn for the Worse

She said, 'What's up with him, the bloody mental idiot?' I said, 'I don't know – I cook, I wash and he doesn't give me nowt for food and because I won't give him no money out of my earnings, this is how he's turned'.

NG

Paying Your Way

You see, Ron, I will say this. Even though he liked to go for a drink – when he got his settlings we always went on the road and got what the kids wanted or anything that needed replacing. But on the other hand, he never came home to a bill unless it had just come in as he was coming home, because I saw to the bills. I paid the way, you know. As I say, you'd walk for miles. I mean, when we went to live up Willerby Road and I was having Christine, and I walked the full length down Hessle Road to get the groceries and such as on to Willerby Road, 'cos that was the way you did it.

KF

Dock Races

You used to go down, you used to call it Dock Races on Thursday. You used to see all the women going down with their kids on a Thursday, for the wages. When I first got married it was four pound ten a week wages…I'd been earning more than that at Woolworths…But sometimes I've been without wages. 'Cos he'd come in from sea, sign off a ship, and wouldn't sign on the dole. I used to have to go to me father and ask him to lend me wages and that's why I went out to work. It didn't suit Albert, but I said, 'No. You'll have to buck your ideas'. I had it rough, I did have it rough, like a lot more Fleetwood women, but you made the best of it. You couldn't [say] – 'I'm packing up and going back to me mothers'. So, eventually we got a nice home together and I was working for these two doctors and I got pregnant with Roy. It was after Roy was born that things started looking up a bit. I give up full time – I'd gone to work at the geriatric hospital…he [my husband] said you can go on the condition that you only do part time.

AS

Alice Stizaker. 'In those days you had to give up work at Woolworths when you married'.

Please Yourself

Oh yes, he used to say, 'Do as you like. Please yourself'. He didn't put his foot down or anything like that. And I was pleased I kept on 'cos I needed it after he died didn't I?

FW

Booze Money

They haven't much money to go far. It isn't a lot of money when you haven't got a man to keep, but nevertheless, when he came in he wanted his booze money and if he didn't pick up anything much well, I mean, the wife, of course naturally supplied it. He wanted a percentage of his wages I should imagine. They had families to bring up. It was hard work. They used to think I was wonderful 'cos I was working, but I was very independent, you see. I've always had to be independent. I had to bring him up before I ever got married to Alan. And I had all the bills to pay. If you've all the bills to pay, my dear, you're on your own, aren't you? You're independent, aren't you?

FW

Secret Bank Book

I used to save as much as I could out of my wages. I had a secret bank book that he didn't know about. I think a lot of wives did. If they gave you so much money a trip, whatever they picked up…I paid everything…I always had a straight household.

AS

Skipper's Wife

I was lucky. I got married to a skipper and got my £10 a week as regular as clockwork. It came by registered post. But, with me working, I used to save that money so, when he came in dock if he wanted anything I used to give him money, you know, take it out the kitty. He'd give me it back and if he used to make a lot of money he used to give me part of his earnings.

FW

Negotiated Settlement

When we went to work we gave the wage packet to me mother and she gave you pocket money back. We weren't allowed to open our wage packet. Once she stopped taking your wage packet she negotiated your board.

VS

Owing

If we'd have had any more children and it'd been a boy, I was always threatening him with the name Owen, 'cos he was always at my mother's borrowing. Owing this. 'I'll pay you next trip, ma.'

CS

Domesticity

The only part my father took in the home and this is when he left the sea was gardening and he deeply resented having to do that. All our lives at any other time he never washed a pot, dried a pot, made a bed, cut the grass – no part in the home life whatsoever. We as young children at an early age had to do a lot of things. But no he took no part at all. I mean that was the typical Victorian male I suppose and I don't think that

Freda Whitelam, aged twenty-one.

51

was peculiar probably to sea. I mean that was the generation when the woman stayed at home.

LS

Nothing's Changed

There was always something to do, wa'nt there? Well, washing… Well, you know don't you? That hasn't changed, has it?

MR

Twelve-hour Shift

When I went in the canteen I'd sometimes work from six o'clock in the morning to half six at night and he'd have me tea ready for me when I come home, or he'd hoover up. Some said, 'Ooh, mine wouldn't do that'. But I think most would.

GH

No Time to Moan

When they was coming in dock everything used to be spick and span and as soon as they hit the house it was [like] a bomb had hit it, you know what I mean? It was just as they was. You didn't say a lot to them because, with them being at sea…like now I would say to him, do you have to leave this here and that there, but you didn't seem to bother. You just seemed to take it that they'd drop everything as they come in. You didn't

have time to moan, not really.

MR

A Woman's Work

I never went out while he was at sea either. I didn't have time. When I used to come home I used to bake and get ready for the next day, and I was up at four o'clock in the morning, ready to get up. I mean, I didn't have no time…and I knitted. I used to have knitting needles – I used to knit coats and dresses for my girl and jerseys for the lads. I was always knitting.

MG

Spick and Span

I've known him scrub all the kitchen and that out. I think a lot of fishermen did that. Like scrubbing. Because, they was used to it, wasn't they? They used to scrub everything down when they was coming home and what-have-you. But I know my mam used to say he got on her nerves because if he had a trip off he used to clean brasses, scrub and clean and she used to say, 'He used to get on my nerves'. I always remember her saying that…It just seemed a way of life.

MR

Soft Touch

He was always a soft touch; I mean he'd come home. I will give him

June Hewitt (centre) and work mates take a break.

his due, he'd come home. Say we were going out. Well he'd get the tea ready while I bathed the kids…or he'd press the clothes while I was seeing to tea. We shared it. I will say that we shared it.

KF

Meat and Potatoes

I had David at home at Ladysmith Road and he cooked a dinner. Just meat and potatoes, no greens, no Yorkshire pudding and my mum come and she said 'Is he looking after you alright?'…'I've just give her a big cooked dinner!'

JH

The Bag Wash

I remember the bag wash on the corner of Regent Street when I was a kid. Taking me dad's big heavy gear to the bag wash. That was an experience in itself. I mean the laundrette's nothing on it! All these women in turbans and aprons. Like overall aprons. Floral tied, you know, at the back. Big pockets. Big busty ladies, washing the laundry. The things they had in that place to wash with. It was unbelievable. Coppers and ironing and all sorts of things. I don't know half of them. I mean they must have been there all day to do it.

CS

'In dock'. Grimsby north wall, 1948.

Washing Day

I have seen my mother get up in morning, go and prepare the veg for dinner before she went to work, go to work…come washing day, she would go do her washing before she started her day's job and when she came home on a dinner time she would knock a batch of bread up to be raising when she came home and that day when she came home on a night-time she used to come home with a big dolly tub of washing and that bread was ready to have with eggs, tomatoes and bacon for tea. Nowadays people would not stand the hours for the women. Mainly for what they had to do beforehand and come home. If they went to the wash house they used to get a four or five o'clock boil and come straight home and go to work and in between come home in dinner hours to prepare your food and coming home at night-time. I remember my father, there was a particular neighbour and she used to give her husband – one night a week – mussels and bread and jam and my mum had done the same as she had had a really busy day…'Don't ever do that, don't come them tricks'. He had to have his cooked meal. To this day if I pass a bakery and smell hot bread it brings all them memories back.

KF

Turn Around

When he came in dock his washing would always be put into soak, 'cos he had three sets. She always had a set clean, a set soaking and a set he had with him.

VJ

54

CHAPTER 5

Mother tongue

Hull trawler, *Ocean Spirit*, leaves Lock Pit, Hull.

Call of the Sea

The youngest one, he did two pleasure trips on his ninth birthday…'cos they baked him a cake…I think he had two pleasure trips but he usually says to his dad 'I don't know how you stuck it out there'.

MR

Don't Go

He took them to sea. The eldest boy Stuart – the one that's a sea captain – he's in South Africa with the big boats. He took him to sea at twelve. He was a born fisherman. He was there helping to gut the fish with them and all that. It was in him. It was all he ever wanted to do. So when he left school at fourteen and wanted to go to sea, I begged him not to go 'Please don't go. There's other things in life apart from fishing'. I said, 'You don't want to be a fisherman'. Anyway, he got a job on the fish docks, in the fish houses, washing the fish and gulling and skilletting and that. I said to him, 'we'll get you a motor bike'. He hadn't had it a few weeks and he [my husband] came home one day and buggered off. He'd left home. Gone somewhere and left us without any money. I was papering the flat above and he come to me and he said, 'Mum', and I said, 'Why aren't you at work?' And he said, 'Mum, I'm going to sea. I've been and signed on', and he'd been down and got himself a ship. I said, 'Oh, no. I don't want you to go', and he said, 'You need my wages'. I didn't. I couldn't stop him. He went. I'll never forgive him [my husband] for that.

The other one went to school at Havelock. He did his eleven plus and passed all his exams and everything. It was a grammar stream school then, attached to it was the grammar department. And Martin got into the grammar department. He was very, very clever. I thought, 'Oh, I've got one who's going to be a professor or something'. I was kidding myself, wasn't I? Out papering – working like hell to get the money, comes home, there's this letter waiting for me. Opens this letter and it's from the head of the grammar section. Please can I make an appointment to see him. I thought, 'What the hell's going on?' but I never said anything. When I get there he gets me in this office and sends for the lad to sit alongside of me. 'I understand your lad wants to leave grammar section because you want him to work to keep you'. I nearly fell off the bloody chair. I said, 'I beg your pardon. Who wants the money?' He said, 'He tells me he's going to work for wages to keep you'. I said, 'Tell him the truth. Who gives you money? I run a car. I give him money' I said, 'I go three jobs a week, what do I want his money for?' When it come, he didn't know how to tell me that he wanted to leave school so he thought he'd do it that way. Then of course, he left the grammar school and he went. He got on the tugs. I said, 'Don't go fishing. Do something else, but not fishing. Go in the Merchant Navy if you want'. Anyway, he joins the tugs. Well, he isn't satisfied, is he? Not enough money, is it? No. Back to sea. Off he goes. And he's still at it. So that's two lads still at it…hated it. Never slept for weeks. I begged and prayed for them not to go…I can't explain it. It's like…it's like the old saying, 'sons following fathers', isn't it? Well, it's happened. It's in them. They're never happy unless they're in that bloody water.

MG

In the Blood

I said, 'Why don't you go to Navigation school – go in the Merchant Navy'. But, no, he wanted to go fishing. Even their dad, at first, he didn't want any of them to go to sea. They went because – there must be something in the blood. I made sure me lads got their mates ticket.

AS

Dad's Footsteps

At first, I didn't want John to go. No, as he grew older I didn't want John to be a fisherman. I sort of changed my mind. He'd say, 'No mam, I'm going'. I'd tried to encourage the two of them for fishing. I thought it was right to follow their dad's footsteps but I wouldn't push them into it. Do you know what I mean? Wouldn't demand it. John was more quiet and reserved than Paul, the littlest one. He got near the sea he was determined. He was getting after fish you see. I've brayed him many a time for being at the fish quay. I was petrified he'd go after he came home from school or he'd go even before he went to school if he got the chance. 'I just watched the boats, mam'…that's what he'd do.

LD

In the Navy

Me two eldest brothers was both Navy. Me youngest brother – he went to sea. He went to sea with Roy. Me mam would never eat for the first two or three trips – all the while he was away, she'd never eat. Because she was so…well, you could imagine how she felt, you know. He was her baby and that was it, you know. But he died at thirty-nine.

MR

Pleasure Trips

I'd never been on me own…I went to me mothers the next day, well, 'You've made your bed, you lie on it'. Then I got pregnant…my eldest lad. I lost him four year ago. He was washed away from Mallaig. Never got him back. I had three sons. Peter was a fisherman. Robert – he went to sea for one trip and didn't like it. Richard, the third son couldn't wait to leave school to go to sea. They used to go on pleasure trips.

AS

A Matter of Choice

He used to go on freezers and he would be away for what, six weeks? I had two sons…they both went fishing…I didn't get any choice. Alan went to nautical school and his dad signed the papers for him, and then his father died but he still went to nautical school. Then he went on a pleasure

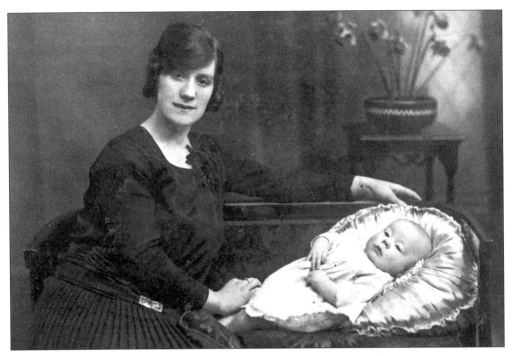

Beatrice Young with first son, Fred. Beatrice was also the mother of Vera Smith.

trip and then started going to sea. He loved it.

FWo

Matriarchy

I think my mum had a harder life and I don't mean that because of my dad. But, me mum had her mum living with her and then she died and she had two sisters and me dad used to buy their clothes and they looked after them. So me mam went to work. Me mam, was a fish washer, my mam was. She could do anything, my mam. She used to go and stipple walls. She used to lay people out. She used to go around with the midwife delivering babies. Oh, she's done everything, my mam did.

MR

Yours for Keeps

In the older days you could not get baby minders, I could not say to my mum will you have the kid all day, because she would say, 'No you have had it, you look after it'. When my husband was fishing she did come one night and sit with them while we went out, but we had to pay her, not like nowadays.

RS

Rod of Iron

You see, my aunty…She was really very strict with me mother. I mean, they took the eldest boy off her. They took him to live with them because she had her second one very quickly and aunty Anne felt she couldn't cope with the two. So, they took Fred – only in the next street – but they took him off her and she didn't get him back till he was seven. It was me dad that got him back. Don't get me wrong – they saw him every day. Interestingly enough my eldest brother thought he was illegitimate until two years ago. He thought that my mother wasn't married and that was why…but she was married. Aunty Anne, eldest sister, decided mother couldn't cope so she took him away 'cos she didn't have a little boy, she only had girls. Aunty Anne said that was the right thing to do. Aunty Anne ruled her with a rod of iron.

VS

Over the Garden Wall

I used to take the cot every trip, every time he went away, put it over the wall to me mam's and used to stop at me mam's. Two [kids] – well you couldn't do that then. So you sort of had to stay in your own place…I still used to eat at me mam's and what have you.

MR

No Daughter of Mine

They found out he'd got thrombosis so he was back in hospital again and I'd gone down docks and his daughters wasn't working down docks, so he told me mum at the hospital. She come home and said, 'You've got to leave that job, Norma' I said, 'Why?' She said, 'Your dad doesn't want you working down there'. I said, 'Well there's nowhere else to get any money from, mam, and I've got to

help you'. So that's why I stopped down docks.

NG

A Way of Life

The girls that married the fishermen accepted the life. They were out for ten days if they were on a small 'un, if they were on the big 'un they were out for fourteen to sixteen days. It was a life that they accepted. I'll be quite honest with you, I haven't much time for those women who whinge about their husbands being away. They should have been married to deep sea trawlermen and they weren't as bad as the Grimsby men who were away for three to four weeks up around Iceland.

FWo

Births, Marriages and Deaths

And then the war came. There was men came from Grimsby and Hull…Lumpers to work here in Fleetwood and they were going round knocking on doors and of course, me mother took two in. And then there were these Danes that she took in. She never turned anybody away. She was an 'auntie', auntie Rachel to everybody round the area. She was there for births, marriages and deaths. Anybody wanted laying out – me mother went!

AS

Mother's Daughter

My mother always had this thing that the seven kids – three boys, four girls – that none of us would have that sort of life. We are, all three of us, trained nurses. She made us go to school, she made us go to night school. She taught us how to cook, sew, knit. But her aim was, we should have 'careers'. We would not be dependent like she was. That was a big thing with me mum. I think in a different generation she would have been a very independent lady. She lost her father, her mother died when she was about four. She was put into the Sisters of Mercy Convent and brought out when she was old enough to work, which was about thirteen, fourteen. She

Vera Smith's grandmother, Elizabeth Young.

always wanted to be a teacher, you see, but because of the situation she couldn't be a teacher. I admire her for it now, I resented it, I think, at the time – when all the children were playing out and we had to go to night school. I think we all resented it, the girls particularly but now [when] we look back I'm glad she had the foresight. She always used to say, 'You'll be able to be independent'. And, I suppose we all are. She never, ever said that she never wanted us to marry fishermen, but, I think she may have been cleverer than what we thought because of what we did and what we were made to do with education and things like that. We weren't allowed to go to pubs. I've never been in a pub on Hessle Road because you didn't meet nice girls in pubs.

VS

End of a Shift

The last four years of my mum being alive I used to leave Ross's at six in the morning. I used to be home for about ten past. I used to go straight to her flat…clean her teeth for her and get her up and she'd have a drink of tea. I'd get her to the bathroom. While she was getting dressed I'd do her breakfast for her…and then I'd say, 'You all right, mam? Going home. I'll see you later'.

NG

Not to be Repeated

I wouldn't have liked any of them [my daughters] to marry fishermen. I think the life was too hard. It was very, very hard. I wouldn't want them to go through what I've been through. Well, they've seen it as they've grown up. They've realised it.

DM

Road to Nowhere

I was at work at fifteen, but we weren't working in the environment. Nobody was allowed to go in a factory. None of us were allowed to work in the factory or fish house or Metal Box or Smith and Nephews. My mother thought it was the road to nowhere. I mean, a lot of people would object to me saying that but in her opinion that was the road to nowhere. You were living on Hessle Road and working on Hessle Road so she got us out, particularly the girls. Looking back, you can admire her really, because in the '40s and '50s that was very forward thinking, don't you think? I don't think me sisters ever came in contact with fishermen. Not that she had anything against them, but she didn't want us to have her life, so you can only deduce from that, that her life couldn't have been all that good.

VS

No Respect

I was married and had three sons and my mother still didn't like me going in the pub. 'Have you no shame? Have you no respect for yourself? What does he want to go taking you in a pub for?'

AS

Tradition

He was…a dominant one that has to be in charge – but it is not put up with nowadays. Them days really a lot of the wives did as it was a good thing, it's passed down from mother to daughter such as, but to be quite truthful a lot of the wives could not afford to go anyway, could they?

KF

A Shilling a Week

My mother always had a little secret drawer upstairs and said, 'if it's only a shilling a week, put it away'. And it was always instilled in me about insurance. That was the way I'd been brought up. My mother used to say, 'Don't you put ropes round that lad's neck'. Do you know what that means? It meant to get them in debt. A lot of women, they never paid the things while their husband was at sea. They had to wait for the husbands coming in before they paid it. Well, what happened if their husband made a dud trip? They couldn't pay it, could they? My husband said 'Well, I've nothing like that'. I said, 'Well, you ought to thank God'.

AS

Carol Spriggs with her mother, at her daughter's wedding.

Dinner on the Table

She used to say 'Get yourself home, Vera. Get the table set. Put your knives and forks on the table and if his dinner's not ready he'll think it is'. I still do it. I still set the table. I've always got it in me mind, 'Well, the dinner's not ready but he'll think it is'. And he doesn't give a knack whether his dinner's ready or not!

VS

Self Sufficient

My girls have been very self sufficient, too. I think I have made them more self sufficient than they would've been had their father been here.

CS

CHAPTER 6

Relationships

Molly Roberts with husband-to-be, Roy.

Molly Roberts (right) takes a break with work mates.

Courtship

When I worked at the clothing factory, I used to walk home and he used to live in that area and he used to be going out with his mates. Well, you know, a gang of lasses leaving work and a load of lads all shouting to each other. Then you get talking. It was pictures then…I wouldn't have dreamt of going in a pub. Me father drunk enough and he used to say to me, 'If I ever see you in a pub, you'll get the biggest showing up'. So I was very wary. We used to go on a lot of outings then. You know, bus trips from work or from the street. He was in a football team. Maybe a football outing. We used to go for a drink out at Louth or Mablethorpe – that area. I'd go to the pubs then, 'cos I knew me dad wasn't round there. But he drunk enough for us all!

GH

On the Corner

I left school and went to work at Woolworths – it was a good job then. I ended up as supervisor but I started courting Albert. It was a love-hate relationship. I hated him when he'd had a drink and then he used to come and stand on the corner. 'Can you come to the pictures?' Me parents were strict. You had to be in for half ten on a night. Daren't go in the pub. Used to sneak in and have a port and lemon.

AS

Next Door-but-one

Cos me dad got blown up in the dock here – when I was three. My brother was eight months old and my mam had four more, you know. I always said I'd never marry a fisherman and then I went to live next door-but-one to him. I knew he was a fisherman. I was friendly with his sister and I used to go in their house but I never really went in when he was there. It wasn't the fact that I wouldn't go in when he was there but it never arose. I used to go in and out and I never seemed to be there when he was there.

MR

First House

While they were ashore…well, sometimes you went to Blackpool. While we were courting there was always three or four couples went around together. We used to go to the First House Palace at Blackpool and then we'd go for a drink. But the last train was Blackpool at half past ten.

AS

Return a Favour

I used to work most of the time, anyway, when Roy was away, when I was courting him. I used to ask him sometimes if I could have landing day off, and depending on how many he'd got off he'd let you. He used to say, 'Don't forget, I want this favour back' and I'd probably work every night. But when they was busy there I used to go in at ten in the morning and didn't used to come home while ten at night.

MR

Nights Out

When I was courting I use to enjoy it being at work and waiting for him coming in dock so that we could have the two full nights out, not days because you couldn't get the time off work to be with them all the time.

RS

Taking a Break

He come in from sea and come to go out with her husband and asked who I was and, then he went off to sea and when he came back he said to Emily's mother, 'Do you think she'd like to go for a night out?' So, she said, 'Yeah, why not. It'll give her a break. We'll look after the baby'. So, we went out and it carried on from there. It was only a matter of a few months then we went into rooms and that's how we got together, you see. So, really, we were thrown together. Yeah. I always said it was a marriage of convenience, we were actually thrown together. I said to him, 'I've got a job to go to.' And he said, 'No, you won't' he said, 'I'll keep you. You stay'. But it wasn't till I married him that he altered. Before that he behaved hisself.

MG

Boy Bosun

I met him when he was fifteen and it was a shame really because all the other boys that you liked or they liked you, they didn't have the money that a fisherman had. They didn't have the money so when Ron came in from sea, he was the only boy that had a car in Fleetwood. You was, sort of trapped really in a way because you were going out with somebody who could take you out and give you a good time and all the other lads were, just, apprentice joiners and he was a mate, well, he was a boson when I met him they used to call him the 'Boy Bosun' Then he took his mate's ticket when I would be about sixteen and then we got married.

PW

A Place to Meet

When you got married at Woolworths then, you couldn't stay on, you had to leave. They wouldn't keep you on in them days. [I felt] a bit annoyed actually, I'd been there since leaving school and I was supervisor. All the Deckies used to come round Woolworths. Toffee was still rationed, biscuits was still rationed, they used to cheque at eight o'clock in the morning all the deckies, they used to come round Woolworths chatting all the girls up.

AS

Sisters

To tell you the truth he was the only boyfriend I have ever had really. His brother was married to my sister and although I didn't know him all that well, I went to baby mind one night for my sister and he was there like and the night he asked if he could take me out and that was it. I had a bit of an idea with his brother being a fisherman and

my sister being married to him like.

RS

Everything Changes

While we were courting. Ooh, how wonderful and all that. But when we got married everything, everything changes somehow or another and you get children on the scene. It gets you down because it's hard enough bringing up children without them.

DM

You Can Tell

The fishermen, they used to come in dock straight into the pub or club. Used to come out and go into these clubs and used to wear suits and the back of the jacket had like pleats in it and the trousers, you could tell they was fishermen if you only saw the jacket. They looked flared but not flares as we know, but they had a little bit of layer in them and they always wore them they never wore overcoats.

VH

Nice Girls

I can't remember what country he came from but he was very dark skinned but he was not a Negro do you know what I mean he could have been anything I don't know. But nice girls didn't go out with coloured people. That's the first time I came up against it. Now if there had been a gang of us and we met in a

66

dance hall and been together all night and come home on our own and say arranged to meet them at a dance hall another time that would have been all right – but if I had let him take me home or take me out I would have been no good. It's the same as if you wore rouge up here, lipstick and that…what they called too much in them days.

JH

Tying the Knot

When his father took him to sea we decided to get married and we nearly didn't get married because he was at sea and we was gonna get married on the Saturday at the Registry Office and the ship just scraped through, just scraped the lock pits else there wouldn't have been no marriage on the Saturday. We'd have had to wait for the next tide to come in and that's too late bec\ause the Registry Office shut at twelve as you know on a Saturday. So we got married and we went in this pub in Central Market and the two, his friend, his best man, took the flowers off, left me and my friend and his friend's wife. He went down dock and he signed off. Signed on the *Boston Fury* on Saturday morning and he went to sea on the Monday. So that was my honeymoon!

EM

Something Better

We'd got engaged and then I broke the engagement before he went to sea and he got shipwrecked. It was about six months later that I got back in with him. There was something there. But me parents, they just didn't want me to get too involved with him. They said, you're throwing your life away and I just said to me dad one day, 'Well, you was a fisherman', and he said, 'Well, there's nothing in it'. He said, 'You want your head reading'. But, you see, you don't take no notice, do you? So I eventually got married in 1950. Me parents didn't come to the wedding 'cos he was a fisherman and they didn't approve. They said they wanted something better for me. I don't know why 'cos me other sister had gone to work in the fish house. My brother went fishing…all my cousins went fishing.

AS

Glamorous granny winner: Edith Mewse, by the seaside.

Freda Whitelam on her wedding day, to skipper Alan Whitelam.

Soldier, Soldier

I was determined not to marry a fisherman but in the end he did go sea. I didn't want to marry a fisherman…I married a soldier and he came out the Army and went fishing. I wasn't very keen but he liked it so he went. My dad didn't give me away at my wedding 'cos he was away at sea. My brother did.

VJ

Hand in Marriage

I always remember when he asked me dad if we could get engaged and me

dad said, 'Yes, but it doesn't mean you can take privileges and I don't want to hear of my daughters name being bandied around the Galley'. He said, 'Your dad. I wish the ground would have opened up!' I said, 'I'd sooner have a good hiding off me dad than a good talking to'. He was a big man, my father.

AS

Eggs in One Basket

He said, 'How about putting our eggs in one basket?', and that is how he proposed. Always a gentleman, he always came round scrubbed clean and a white shirt, you know what I mean? The companionship really was great. We weren't the young silly couple, loving full bloom like when you are young. It's a different cup of tea, isn't it, when you get to our ages?

FW

Going Out/Staying In

They always went out on one of the nights when he was home…and that used to be fine if they went to play bingo which in those days was a big night out. People went to play bingo as groups.

PW

Altogether

When we was out, he used to spend the same as the rest of them, but Roy only had landing day out. A lot of them, they used to get a bus up and we used to go out of town – all the wives and husbands…off the same ship…they used to run loads, like to Louth, Kidby Bridge, all over you used to go and it was nice. Well that was an extra bonus if you went on one of them because otherwise we didn't use to go out, other than on landing day. You was all together. And you got used to know them people and especially if they was in a ship a long while. So, if you see them out we always had the time of day for one another. He used to go down to land then he used to send a taxi up for me. And I would never go in a pub on me own. I used to say to him, 'If you're not there I'm going home' so he used to come out the pub for me. And a lot of the blokes used to do that 'cos a lot of the women wouldn't go in the pubs on their own.

MR

Ladies Present

That was all they talked about – fishing. But, very occasionally they'd slip up and say, 'Oh, excuse me. Ladies present'. You never heard them come out with any foul language.

AS

Lovely Days

Ron liked to go for a drink and he used to like to get to the bar with the other fishermen…so you were left with the other wives to chatter and I think I tend to be a bit of a loner. If he were coming in on a Friday and obviously they couldn't land the ship till the Monday, that was super because as he came in…he'd ring me up from sea and I would say 'Okay, I'll get

Going out. Molly Roberts (left) and friends.

that. And that's what she did – she looked after the kids but when he came home she got her clothes back and he nearly always took her out and she was always very well dressed and glamorous really. She wasn't allowed to drink too much. He used to let her have pale and limes and that was it. Interestingly enough none of his daughters were ever allowed to go in a pub.

VS

Apron Strings

I had the children wherever I went. Where I went they went too and I never did go out on a night-time, it was not the done thing but on the other hand you could not afford to because you could not afford the babysitters to go out, could you?

MR

Congregate

Fishermen's wives used to gang up and congregate together and know one another and they used to go in the pub, sometimes, for a drink while their husband's away. Or sometimes they'd go and play bingo together or the club together, but, you see, I never had time. You imagine. I never had time. So, I just kept me three bairns and meself going.

MG

Vera Smith's mother, Beatrice Bryan, and Fred Young on their wedding day.

everything ready'. I'd book the caravan and then we'd pick the kids up from school and we'd go off and we'd go up to the Lake District and they were lovely days.

PW

Key to It All

She was never allowed to go out when my dad was at sea. He has been known to lock her clothes up so she couldn't go out 'cos he felt that her place was with the kids and not gallivanting out to pubs and things like

Respect

He very rarely, when he was home, went out without my mother. He would get drunk, but he would never be abusive or anything like that. You had a lot of time for him, a lot of respect for him.

VS

Sheikh of Arabic

Mother had people going in and out all the time. She did have friends. My mother used to throw a party. Get me to play the piano for these friends. And they used to make you laugh, 'cos music them days – they used to make their own music. They used to get a couple of drinks down them there and mother used to give them a drop of sherry – get me to sing – get the piano going, they'd say. 'Get this bloody piano going. Play the piano.' And she'd come in with a copper stick – I don't know if you remember the old fashioned copper stick that your mother used – stirred the clothes round in the copper. Wood. One of them, a dustbin lid and a towel round her head and balloons stuck up here. 'I'm the Sheikh of Arabic' and they all used to congregate in this big house – where Stuart is now – and they used to do all the dancing. Me mother used to bake and put fancy cakes and all that on for them. And that's how me mother spent her life.

MG

Customers and staff of The Barrel on a night out.

Tired as Well

One day I went into him at Tank [pub] I'll always remember. It was a gorgeous day. I'd just gone to the end of me tether, I went in and I said, 'Tommy Mersey in there please?' They said 'Yes'. I said, 'Will you tell him his wife's out here please?' I said 'Here's your kids'. He said, 'Well, I've been to sea'. I said, 'Yeah, well, I've had 'em all the time you've been to sea. And I'm tired as well'. And I said, 'You can have 'em for the rest of the day. I'm off'. And I left him with the kids. Well, he couldn't say 'owt – he didn't have a leg to stand on and I only went and sat in the park all afternoon. I thought it was lovely. He started to calm down a little bit after a while. And I said, 'Right – you go out in future you take us and the kids with you'. So he used to do that.

DM

Having a Life

While he was away I had a life. When Graham was away at sea I didn't go to pubs and things but I did all sorts of things. I went to night school, things like that. He never objected to me going anywhere. Never objected to me going out, never objected to me nursing, working. I could work all the hours God sends.

VS

Eureka

She thought one day, 'I'll show him up', so she took his dinner to the club – it was called the Eureka and she took his dinner to him to show him up. He said, 'That was smashing, is there any more?'

OL

Walking Out

He [Albert] was a happy-go-lucky lad. A lot of Fleetwood lads knew him. He used to like to get up on the stage in the Gasworkers Club. They used to encourage him to sing these daft sea songs and I used to say, 'You get up and I'm not staying' and I used to walk out. As I say, when he'd had a drink I hated the ground he walked on.

AS

Dry Dock

My brothers didn't go drinking when home from a trip. Maybe take their wife for a meal. I suppose that was just what you did. They didn't know anything else.

OL

Unwritten

And there was what he called the 'Scrobs', the Danish and so on, and they was all in the same pub and we had real good nights. We'd get used to each other. But on the other hand, each person knew it was an unwritten law – they didn't come and chat your wife up while you'd gone to the bar or gone to the toilet. It was only these people that were on the game. But even they had a code of conduct – they would look after the wife that was left there at the toilet – 'She's married' and they would tell them that she was married – it just wasn't the done thing. You know, that's how it was.

KF

Would You Mind?

He said, 'Do you mind if I go out?' We never went out at night without each other.

FW

Open Prison

If the family had a day's outing or a party at home or some celebration of some sort, or whatever, she was not allowed to go there, not even to a family party. She felt terrible, you know, and we all used to have days out in our younger days and family days out, but she was not allowed to go. Well it was in case she met somebody while we were out. Do you see? They were very closely guarded, their family life.

VH

You're Golden

I went to one or two [parties] but he wouldn't go without me. 'You're golden', he used to say to me. 'You're golden'. 'Cos I didn't argue with him.

FW

Family Ties

When your husband's at sea you don't go out. Not in the pub or anywhere, not even dancing. It was frowned upon. You got the odd one – like the girls of the village. Like in every port, you did. But I didn't. My mother would have hit me, let alone me husband. You didn't do it.

AS

Parlour Tricks

I always remember one day when I came home early. We had a 22 foot lounge and there was about eight or nine skippers. Smoke was in the air and 'oh my God'. I don't drink myself, you know. So I said to him, 'Just a minute, you lads, I'll get the brush', and came in with the yard brush. I always remember skipper Johnstone saying to me, 'Now what you doing, Freda? Now what you up to?' I said, 'I'm just going to sweep all this fish away 'cos I can't get in'. Oh, of course, that was uproar.

FW

Still Watching

I'd been in rooms for six years and then we got this council house and it was like living in no man's land and it got sometimes that it was too far for him to come home. He'd go out towards dinnertime and 'I'll be home at three'. It would be more like eleven or twelve at night, but he'd say that it was too far for him to come home. I used to get annoyed. We'd have rows but I never let him go to sea without I made it up. Never.

AS

Genuine People

I've a tremendous amount of claimants on my books that don't drink and they're churchgoers and they live in modest houses and they've been happily married and there's no domestic violence but unfortunately the media does tend to portray a fisherman as being a loudmouthed, drunkard that, sort of, came in from sea and caused trouble, probably knocked his wife about. To me, it's totally wrong and this is what's being portrayed. I've got them coming in here, complete and utter waste of space but there's a hell of a lot that come in that are very, very genuine people.

JM

Chinese Whispers

I can recall two arguments but I'm sure there were more...He was very possessive of her, very jealous of her. I think that's why he didn't let her go out. And if she was seen talking to anybody, somebody would tell him, 'cos they always did, didn't they?

VS

Two Sides of the Coin

My father was a fisherman, and my uncles were. They didn't go out boozing in pubs. They took a drink in the house with my mother. She never went out to work 'cos they kept her. They would have a drink in the house but they never went out boozing. I thought they was the same as me dad. I didn't realise what the other side of fishing life was like. When I was a young girl, my father was always there, so I didn't know the other side till I married him. But, I'd married him and I stuck by...them days you stuck by what you'd said. Not like today when you can go off and leave them. I had the children then. So, I decided I'd make a home – which I did – and I worked damned hard for it.

MG

Rose-tinted Specs

When women used to see one another they used to talk. Sometimes you used to meet them on the street and they'd say, 'Look at this', and lift their glasses up and they'd got a black eye or something. I think what it is, is when they're out there it's men only and they have to be tough to stand the strain of the seas. 'Cos it isn't a very pleasant job. It's a hard life. I think it made them that they were really tough and they just didn't know how to handle women properly when they came ashore. All they wanted to do was go in a boozer, and they spent their lives in boozers. All the time. Every day.

MG

Lights Out

When me dad was at home if he went to bed at eight o'clock, he'd switch the television off. 'Right, Beat! Bed', and she'd go. She'd go.

VS

No Worries

I tried to make everything, when Ron was home, right, nothing was wrong. Nobody had to worry him, nobody had to say anything – everything was lovely.

PW

Honour and Obey

All the time…my father obeyed her. He thought she was wonderful. He idolised her. Her word was law.

MG

Behind Closed Doors

The fishermen coming home pissed every night and beating their wives up – we never had any of that. It maybe did go on and we didn't see it but my father never beat my mother up, I've never known him raise a hand to her. He was very respectful of women, you see.

VS

Second Place

They had a rough time actually. Some of them prayed for their husbands to get their ship back again because of the violence what there was. And it was all drink orientated or in a lot of cases their wives was second to them going out with a friend. A lot of them going out in suits specially made for them. Going out and the poor wife being left at home with the kids. And they daren't say anything. They didn't know what was coming home to them when their husband came in…some of them had dogs of lives. You'd see 'em and…heart bleeds for them. I wouldn't have wanted that.

KF

What Price?

Me mam's friend's husband – he used to take me mam's friend and me mam to Mark's in town and buy them a new nightie each but not me dad, he never did. As I say, he was a good dad, but not a good husband. Even though he used to take her out and buy her a new nightie and dress, he'd maybe give her a good hiding on a night, where me dad never did. I never remember me mam and dad arguing, never, ever. I

75

The fisherman returns. H273 *Admiral Drake*.

never heard them argue. But, she never got a new dress or new nightie.

OL

From Sea to Shore

A miner goes to work at eight o'clock in the morning and comes home at teatime, and he goes to his wife and he's with her and then he goes to bed. When a fisherman leaves the dock, he doesn't see his wife for three or four weeks. All he sees is men and men live rough. And I mean trawlers before the war never had decent toilets. They've lived rough, so, you can't expect a man to be a gentleman in a matter of three days when he's ashore. It doesn't work. And more so when they've had no drink, perhaps, at sea, and they've come and hit a pub straight away and they're gulping it down as fast as they can get it. They don't know where the bloody hell they are half the time.

MG

Flowers

There was always flowers sent through the tele-max if you'd gone to sea with heated words.

CS

Married Life

I was only home a fortnight after [the] first child was born and I got abscesses. I ended up in hospital for four months. He just used to come in hospital and see me. When I come out of hospital I was terrified to resume a married life. I was terrified and it led to – not parting of the ways – but rows and it was me eldest sister that had a good talk to me and he – Albert must have said something to her husband and he said something to Rachel and she gave me a good talking to. It was funny.

AS

Dog's Life

There was one particular one that I know – her husband's dead and gone now, died a few years ago. Anyway she had a dog's life. Must have had seven or eight kids. I guarantee most her clothes she had to borrow to go out with and he was the man of the house and even when he finished at sea he would take the lights out so that their kids wouldn't waste electric.

KF

Pub Lunch

We was in Rayners and Jimmy Pat came in and he had just his 'jamas' and dressing gown on, so we said 'What's going on?' So he said 'She's hidden me clothes so I can't get out', he said. It was about 12 o'clock at dinnertime, so about quarter of an hour

after that she comes in. She said 'Are you coming home?' And he says real clever like, 'When I'm ready.' So, ever so sedate and lady like she moves the glasses on the table and put the table cloth on, knife and fork and got his dinner out of the bag and he was looking amazed and she said 'There you are darling, I'll see you when you get home'.

RF

Here, There and…

He was anywhere – obviously I couldn't mention the names – but there were a lot like that. There was also a lot that…would get on with these women and they didn't realise these women only wanted them for the wages.

KF

Battle Stations

Well, you fell in love again every time they come in again. You fell in love again. You'd probably have battle stations before they went back – but you always made it up. Unless you've been actually brought up in a fishing family or community, you don't know. If there was a tragedy everybody used to rally round.

AS

Mind Games

He never hit my mother, not that I know of. It was more emotional abuse and drunken abuse but he actually never hit her.

LS

Under the Carpet

The police would be called. They'd probably give him a strict talking to but I can't say there would be the coverage like there is now. Let's face it, its only been in the last few years that they've recognised it is abuse and a woman can say no, whether you're married or not. It is the fact that they [the police] can interfere.

KF

The Odd One

You had the odd family that got nasty. They got belted up and that. There was a few that I knew of. You didn't get counselling, you just stuck it out. You'd see the odd one with an eye or summat, you know, he'd had too much to drink and all the rest of it. But I don't think there was all that many.

AS

Going for Gold

When we got married a lot of people said it wouldn't last and I must say – I wouldn't wish my first few years on anybody. It was traumatic. When you were desperate, you were desperate. That was forty-six years ago.

KF

Something

I don't know how affectionate they were, I've no idea…they just lived together in the house and had this family! You know I've never thought about that. No affection at all…if they did it together when we weren't there, maybe so, but…I don't know, there must've been something.

LS

That Extra Bit

Best part, I think of being married to a fisherman – it was something new. I mean you knew one another but you always found that extra bit. Because you weren't together long enough to find everything and I think it takes a long time anyway, to find each other's ways.

KF

CHAPTER 7
Separation

Hull trawler, *Somerset Maughan*, leaves Lockpit, St Andrews Dock, for a three-week trip.

Waiting Game

They call it Ross House and it was across the road which is now a car park. But it took all the corner up and if I was upstairs working and Roy was going to sea, I could see him going. 'Cos the ships used to come round that way and then go out. They seemed like they used to back up and then go out. I could see him, yeah. If he was going to sea and he walked by I could see him 'cos the factory was all open. So I just used to drop down off the platform and go out the back way and see him off.

MR

Keep It All In

My mum never ever said 'Oh, he's coming home, I'm dreading it' because whatever she thought, she kept it to herself.

LS

Getting to Know You

Fourteen to sixteen days away, two days home and if something was wrong with the ship you always used to think yourself lucky because they could have a couple of days extra. You missed the family side of it that somebody's there to talk to and it was only when Ron became ill and when the children had grown up that you actually really begin to know each other.

PW

Waiting

It was a lonely life married to a fisherman. You don't realise till you are married to one, the anxiety of them going away. Yes, definitely, especially in the winter time, wondering what the storms was like and if they would get back safely. Well if he went deep waters he would be away about twenty days, but sometimes he could only be away for ten or twelve days if it was just in and out sort of thing, but that was long enough because he only got two days in dock anyway.

AS

Reprieve

One of the worst things that ever happened was…Ron's mates with a skipper Reggy Wright and I got the message that five men had been drowned off the ship and you think 'How do I respond to this?', I wasn't crying, I was just…it's like when you're about to get a shock you live with this thinking that you've got to prepare yourself that you could have a shock and at that time I thought, 'this isn't happening' – what I thought could happen. It turned out that there was five of them and Ron was going to go with them to the Isle of Man and Ron didn't go but stayed, fortunately, aboard the ship. They didn't find the bodies for a while…they were all drowned…I remember Ron flying over for the inquest – we hadn't been married all that long then. It was a terrible thing.

PW

Waiting. Edith Mewse and son.

Flat or Calm

You're worried all the while they was away especially if it was windy and that and then I used to say, 'By, I bet you've had bad weather' and he used to say, 'it's been flat or calm'. He used to say 'Don't take what's on shore that it's the same out there'. They did have some bad weather didn't they. Some of the time he was kidding me. I know he was.

MR

All Dressed Up

They used to send you a bouquet of flowers or something, but you would not actually hear from them. Sometimes telegrams saying happy birthday or that. Greetings telegram. I don't think he was overly generous with my mother. She didn't have loads of money but when he came home from sea she did have lovely clothes. She used to have her hats made. He used to like her to have her hats made. And she had a silver fox fur and everything like that. She looked brilliant, I can remember. But when he went back to sea the whole lot went and she was housewife and mother. And she used to spend a lot of the three weeks, almost like she was getting ready for him coming home again. I think she resented some of it 'cos it wasn't an easy life.

VS

All Above Board

There was no man allowed over my front door while he was away – but one chap – I forget his name now – he used to like his crisp frilly shirts and he used to bring them to me – you know, for when he came home. And he had a taxi waiting – and he came in and he'd had his bath and everything – not at my house but just to change his shirts. And he'd leave his other shirts with me. But that was all he was allowed to do. And that was all above board. The kids were there and everything – but that was a done thing.

KF

More than Mad

Well she used to get more than mad with him. Me dad – he'd say to me mother, 'Oh, I'll do two or three trips and have a trip off 'cos I want to see you and the kids'.

CS

Going out, Coming in

It's a hard life for the wives and for the husbands. You don't know when they're going out and when they are coming in. In the winter it gets worse. It's a lonely life for the wives because they are bringing the family up for the fisherman.

LD

On My Own

I remember when I got married I had to iron and starch all these separate collars. I used to knit sea jerseys and the hob stockings. I was brought up like that…I went in rooms and I'd only been married about a week and a well known Fleetwood skipper come to me husband and said, 'I want a deckie, Albert'. He was going to sea early morning…and they come to pick him up and he went and I just sat and broke me heart. I thought, 'I'm on me own. What am I gonna do?'

AS

Never Let Me Know

The only time I worried was when he went on one of the Boston boats. It caught fire down below and he had to sail into Tromso or somewhere. One of the fellas didn't get up and I think he lost one or two, I think…it was on television…they never let me know, the owners never let me know. They should do, shouldn't they?

FW

Loss

I mean, there are a lot of fishermen been lost at sea so we've got the widows, young widows with children on our books, and the mission acts as agent for the Ship Wrecked Mariners Society, the Sailors Families Society, the Seamen's Hospital Society, Merchant Navy Welfare Board and I'm also on the

Sheldon window, Fisherman's chapel, January 1982.

Fleetwood Fishing Vessel Owners Benevolent Fund.

JM

Loch Boystul

I got used to him being at home and then he got the itch and he wanted to go back to sea. His face lit up when the ship's husband come and asked him to join the *Admiral Hawk*. It was funny, he liked a bet on the horses. Not a lot of money. The most he ever bet was a pound and I used to hate going in bookies and he was going to sea the Tuesday morning…he was in bed – I was on earlies and I went upstairs to say 'Ta-ra' to him and take a pint mug of tea up to him and I said, 'I'll see you next trip' and he said, 'I've wrote a bet out…it's for Saturday. A pound each way, Loch Boystul?' Now, talk about coincidence. He was killed seven mile off Loch Boystul. And I put that bet on…I never know if it won. I never went in the bookies to find out, but he was killed seven mile off Loch Boystul. They brought me his sea bag home about a week after he'd been killed and I just looked at it and I said, 'Get rid of it. I can't stand the sight of it'.

AS

Always Looking

You could go to bed and go anywhere and not lock doors. I know a lady, a friend of mine and she lost her son and he was only eighteen – he was a deckie learner. She lived in Mendip Avenue – she moved there. She did live over the marsh then. She never used to lock her doors even when it started to get that people were breaking in. I said to her one day, 'You ought to start locking your doors'. She used to say, 'No 'cos he might come home'. People always thought they was going to come home. It's funny isn't it? But my mum, when

The Widowmaker.

THE WIDOWMAKER

When the widowmaker wind howls up the river
And the sky falls dark and heavy to the roaring of the tide
When you lie awake and listen to the wind blow
And you wish you'd never been a sailor's bride

For wives and mothers all along the coastline
It's another day of darkness and another night of fear
For it's gale force nine and black ice in the Faroes
And December is the deadly time of year

Oh! It's hard to be a mother and a father
A lonely woman trying hard to rear a growing lad
And your heart sinks every time he tries to tell you
He wants to go to sea just like his Dad

And in between the kissing and the cursing
You try to build a home where they can grow up straight and free
But there's no way you can keep him there forever
And you know someday you'll lose him to the sea

When your man comes home with money in his pocket
It's like the sun comes shining through the clouds and through the
And the time has come to do your share of living
In two days time he's outward bound again

And the laughing and the singing and the drinking
Are chances to forget the nights you laid alone and cried
And tonight you'll be a Queen but come tomorrow
He's sailing on the early morning tide

When the widowmaker wind howls up the river
And the sky falls dark and heavy to the roaring of the tide
When you lie awake and listen to the wind blow
And you wish you'd never been a sailor's bride

John Co

she lost me dad – and anyone that knows me mum will tell you this – from six o'clock when she used to put me and my youngest brother to bed, my mam used to stand on her front. On the gate – like that – and she just used to stand and people used to come by and she used to stand and have a natter. And she didn't used to go back in the house, only if we cried or anything. She never came back in the house until one of my elder brothers or sisters went in. But I always used to think she was looking. She was always looking. I think when you haven't got anything to show that they've died it must be, one of the weirdest things, don't you? I remember me mum talking about when they went to the memorial thing…there was three ships blown up the same day. And everybody was there but she said you had nothing there, nothing. Like you do when you go a funeral. She said it was this big service. All these people was here, devastated, but there was nothing to grieve. If you understand. It was nothing. And I imagine that you must wonder all your life, mustn't you?

MR

Best of Friends

I don't even remember what my brother looks like without getting a photograph out. We fought like hell but we were the best of friends because he was one of the kindest people, he was just so kind. We were always at home together we went to school together. As we grew, sort of our early teens and whatever, we went our separate ways in that Johnny had his friends and I had

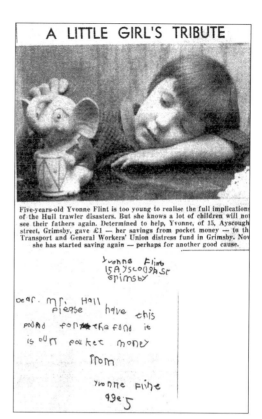

A LITTLE GIRL'S TRIBUTE

Five-years-old Yvonne Flint is too young to realise the full implications of the Hull trawler disasters. But she knows a lot of children will not see their fathers again. Determined to help, Yvonne, of 15, Ayscough street, Grimsby, gave £1 — her savings from pocket money — to the Transport and General Workers' Union distress fund in Grimsby. Now she has started saving again — perhaps for another good cause.

'A Little Girl's Tribute', *Grimsby Evening Telegraph*, 9 February 1968.

my friends but I suppose, because of our history together, we were always there for each other and we were always close.

LS

On the Mines

When me dad got lost – well he got blown up outside here – in the river, he was. On the mines. They was only in the Humber and it was funny because she was waiting for him coming in because me nana had died. She'd bought him a black hat, you know. Oh, and then they used to wear the black armbands then, didn't they? And she'd got all them ready for him and he never come back. So she lost me nana, me dad and his mother in three weeks of one another.

MR

Mr Chapel

When a trawler went down, certainly at Constable Street school, we were all taken into the assembly room 'cos we never knew which trawler had gone down or who'd gone down on it. Mr Chapel used to come from the Bethel with the notification and if it was your dad your mum came to sort you out and take you home and whatever.

VS

Not Knowing

I didn't know and his wife didn't know that he'd been drowned, it was in November, and I'm showing her a Christmas cake over the fence that I'd made and two men walked up the path and just said to her 'Can we have a photograph of your husband?' and she said 'Whatever for?' she didn't know…but they knew.

PW

The Town Grieved

I can remember, he was fishing and his wife stood on the quay waiting for him to come up watching him come in and the ship hit a mine. It blew up. Nearly always at Christmas you would

Fishermen's Mission, Grimsby, 1965.

get a ship sunk. The town grieved. One ship, they nearly all lived around one another.

MGb

Carrying On

We was going to get married at the end of May and he died on 11 May and I just carried on with work – brought me children up.

NG

Too Late

It got a little bit easier. But, you see, after it got easier, about eighteen months after that he'd gone. He started to realise, 'I should have been better to you'. But there's not a lot I can do. It's too late.

DM

Crying Inside

It was just devastating. The whole world died. I've never looked for anyone else. I talk about him and inside I'm crying. I miss him as much as ever. I couldn't have brought another man into the home to take his place. 'Cos they could never have matched up, anyway. They'd have been living in his shadow. If my dad hadn't been there and me mam being so strong, I couldn't think how I would have coped, how I would have gone on. The day they lost their dad, my dad was down. He said carry on

as normal. 'Go down to the shop and get some extra milk for your mam and get a paper for me'. So they went to the shop.

CS

Hang On

I used to go to service sometimes on a Sunday if I could make it. I'm not a religious person but I believe. I always have. Well, you've got to otherwise what can you hang on to? It helped me.

DM

Fairy Tale

This massive bouquet, this great big box of chocolates came with this tele-max. Of course, things went on then as normal. But then, he never went out but he took one of them with him. That's the annoying part. About two years before I lost him, he started to reform. I think that's the hardest part. And for the last two years of his life was the happiest. It was like a fairy-tale. He realised. He thought he was going to lose us, so he woke up, if you will. Not that he was bad before that. He wasn't.

CS

Twelve Month's Wages

He went to sea that Tuesday morning. I was helping a friend at her laundrette, her husband had died that morning in Fleetwood Hospital. Mr Gillmore, from Mission, come and told

The 'new' Seaman's Mission, Grimsby, 1965. This is no longer in use, the mission office having returned to the North Wall.

me Albert had been killed at sea. He just stood in the doorway and the assistant was with him and I just looked at him and I can remember saying, 'Who is it? Albert or Peter?' He said, 'It's Albert'. They took me home. I said, 'What's happened?' He said, 'The rope has whiplashed' and I just wanted to know if he'd been chopped in two and they said as far as they know, he hadn't. And that was off the West Coast of Scotland. It was the following week that he was buried. He was buried as a fisherman because he'd been born and brought up a Roman Catholic, even though we got married in my church. And, I'd started going back to the Mission here on a Sunday afternoon to sing along. In the July my eldest brother hung himself. He hadn't turned for me

sister-in-law but he was buried from the Catholic church but the Mission had been to see her and they said they would have a little service on the Sunday afternoon, and we went and I just said, 'I'm coming back', 'cos we used to go on a Sunday night when we were kids. They called it the Bethel, then, and I started going every Sunday afternoon and I really enjoyed it. I found great comfort, it was a lovely little chapel and I had a plaque put on the wall for him and I give a donation. I had to fight for money. My brother-in-law fought – he was a shop steward at the ICI and all I kept saying was, 'I don't want money off anybody. I've got plenty of insurance'. But, I did get money off them. The equivalent of twelve months wages 'Take it or leave it'. There was an enquiry. There wasn't a mark on him…on his hands. And my dearest wish is that I could have just got me son back to put with him. Terrible…Naturally… 'Is it my husband or is it my son?' When things like that did happen it was terrible. I had a lot of support. I've still got me letters and cards. I had 249 letters and sympathy cards. Everybody – ex-fishermen – they turned out.

AS

Work Through it

Before I had to start looking after mum, I think that it gave me summat to do after losing Albert and with Dawn being so young – living off social security – I didn't want that. Well, I thought, the only thing is work, get extra money so they can have the same as other kids have.

NG

Silver Wedding

I don't think you actually thought they'd never come back. You'd have done your head in, wouldn't you? I loved Albert and I still love him. He's still here…I had me silver wedding.

AS

We'll Meet Again

I think really that's what helped me get through. Hoping one day that we'll all meet again…that's what made me get through my life. I can pretend sometimes, you know?

CS

Storms of Life

There's one of the old hymns, *Will Your Anchor Hold in The Storms of Life*. I picked that for Albert's funeral service and, I've always said, my anchors held quite a few times.

AS

Splitting?

He hit me in the street. Knocked me against the kerb and split all me head open. They took me to the

Stowing the nets. Modern fishing methods, early 1970s.

hospital. Bandaged all up. So me daughter…she went and fetched her [my mother] and when she see it…she picked up the brolly and she tried to beat his brains out. On top of that he run away and left us. He left me to fend for meself and the three bairns and he was missing for three [months]. The police here was going to drag this dock 'cos they thought he drowned himself. He hadn't. He'd done a bunk. He'd gone out for a pint and never come back. Well, two or three times…we'd fallen out. I'd had him to court. He always wanted to come back. Ninety-nine per cent of the law was for the man, not like it is today. But I had three babies – three kids. Me mam, she said, 'Well, you've made your bed you must lay on it'. So, I said, 'Oh well, in that case I've got to go back'. So, that was another dollop. Then me mam was taken ill. I had to go back to help look after me mother. He didn't like it. Flew off his temper. Smashed the clock. Smashed the furniture up, got the sheets off the bed. Put all me clothes, the baines clothes in and dumped 'em in me mother's front garden. So, I went to the law again. They got hold of him and he said, 'No, I'll behave meself'. He never did. So, it hasn't been honey.

MG

Grin and Bear it

I mean nowadays if you separate they go to the council and they either have these emergency hotels or they have some form of shelter. They didn't have none of that then – I mean, to be quite truthful you didn't know the procedures. And you had to grin and bear it or if you was lucky enough to have brothers or that, then they would come and put things straight for you…really it hooked on you. You made your bed and you laid on it. And that was it. But some, they was battered to hell. I mean, it's heart breaking to think they was allowed to get away with it. The ones that have probably been dogs to their wives – and now they totally rely on their wives for looking after them and comfort in their old age. But I suppose it's like everything else – they're young, reckless and they don't give a damn about anything else, really. In that kind of life, as I say, they was home for two days, so they lived their lives to the full. You could see a lot of them the relief that their husband had actually gone back because a lot of them were safe again for three weeks and they could laugh again themselves.

KF

Making a Stand

Right, he'd been home for a week and something had happened to the ship and he started to decorate the living room. And he had this friend who was working ashore… 'Oh come on, we'll go for a drink' and he'd call for him when he was in the middle of decorating. I said, 'Right that's it. You carry on and lead your life'. That's what I said 'Right that's it. I'm leaving you if you go out today. You've promised to decorate the living room. I'm leaving you.' So right, I did. I went to the bank and went to me dad at Liverpool and me aunties. I never even told me mum and at this point me mum was working at the Mission. So he went to the Mission and said, 'Ma, where's Carol and the kids?' 'I don't know. Isn't she at home?' Me dad rang me mum later at the Mission to say where I were and I was all right and the kids. I stayed from the Wednesday and my dad brought me home on the Friday 'cos Basil was ready for sea then. The ship was ready. I came home. The decorating had been done. The storage radiators had gone out. He'd gone and got me a new gas fire. It brought him to his senses. The kids thought they was having a whale of a time. They had a holiday with granddad.

CS

Break Away

I'm not saying everybody was innocent but there was a lot of innocent people out there. Naive, I would say, not innocent, and the stress was too much – the financial side, and they had to break away. Well, everybody knew, didn't they? If you remember then, the divorces used to be in the paper and it was shocking to hear that. They really looked down on you. 'Did you see so-and-so's divorce in the paper?' I think a lot of people stuck at their marriages because – it was a situation where, where could they go? There wasn't the houses…there wasn't the finance there. And really, the separation and divorces were looked down on even by the judicial service. I mean, if it was a woman seeking a divorce out, really, she wasn't classed very highly. But we had one judge here. He hated fishermen. He really hated fishermen and if they went down there you could guarantee that he'd be on the side of the woman because, it was the name that fishermen had – irresponsible and such as. To a certain extent, you're talking about young kids that got married. I think many more people would have divorced, don't you? Had there been the facilities that you've got now. You either grew with it or you got thrown by the wayside.

KF

Back for Good

They argued all the time, that's what the house was, it was always arguments. I remember saying to my mother when he was at sea 'You've made your choice – you could leave him' and when my nana died she left my mum a lot of money and my mother was sixty-two then so I said 'Well, why don't you go?' and she never did.

LS

Choosing to Stay

I used to say 'Well, you've got a choice, you've decided to stay'. And I know there's a generation where you stay married regardless of what your lifestyle was like but she'd no children at home, she'd been well able to take care of herself because she'd maintained the home while he was at sea, she'd paid the bills and she chose to stay.

VS

Rain on Me

Then when he come ashore it took him ages. He had two goes at it and went back to sea. The last time he came ashore he went to work at Dixons Paper Mill and every day he used to come home for his dinner and I bet you every day for the first month it poured down with rain. He used to think it only rained on him. The first six months – every day I told him to pack his bags and get back to sea. I didn't really mean it. Like I said, when it was raining, it only rained on him…he used to come in and stand there and say, 'I'm wet through' and I used to say, 'Oh, and it's not rained on anybody else?' Oh, it was hard. Oh, it really was…yet I really wanted him to stay at home and he really wanted to stay at home. I think that's why he stuck to it.

MS

Do as I Please

I'd had a few years; six, seven years doing exactly what I wanted, albeit nothing wrong…I come and go as I please. If I wanted to stay at work a bit longer I'd stay. Of course he came home and I suddenly found that I had to cook dinner and things like that and I did resent it – initially. I'd had six years of doing my own thing, if you like. I didn't do anything wrong but I always felt I had the freedom.

VS

Separate Lives

Although he's here today – he's sat in the back – I mean, he's never gone without. He's been well looked after. He's still well looked after. But, it has been a terrible life. Could have had a better one, but what's the good of moaning? Too old to do anything about it now. So, I've had more black eyes than counting on your fingers. I know you can't believe it looking at me, but it's true. Yes, yes. I live in the front and he lives in the back today. He's not allowed in here with me. I cook and look after him but that's all. And my children never forgive him. They come to see me and speak to him. It's a funny life, you see.

MG

The Living Years

I got married three years after Ron died and I became widowed again six months later. I would say that I spent more time with my second husband in spite of being married only six months in total time than I had with my husband in thirty-seven years of marriage and that is sad, isn't it? Ron developed cancer in the bladder and we were together then for eighteen months and he said to me 'Do you know I've only just begun to know you'. That sounds ironic, doesn't it, after five children and thirty-seven years of marriage.

PW

Mam at Work

I always remember our Paul – I was at work. After he'd finished his fishing Ron had said to the bairn, 'Who's the boss in here?' so he said, 'Well you are when me mam's at work, aren't you, dad'. Because that had always been the role. You were mother and father. You were the organiser...I don't think you always enjoyed it.

KF

Giving It Up

I used to moan about the kids being a handful, three boys and a girl and he said, 'Alright if I can get a job I will give it up'. He had no trouble in getting a job so he just gave it up. At first it was alright, but as time went on you got fed up of seeing each other and, of course, I went to work at Findus at night-time six till ten. I was there two years before we were made redundant like and went back on the days like, but he got a job on the dustbins and he's been there ever since, that's twenty-eight year now. He loved it, yeah he loved it, it was hell of a difference, in the working, for meals and weather-wise he felt more safe. Because he had a regular wage and he knew what we had to live on and what we had to spend, whereas when they were fishing it was a very poor wage for what they did and the hours they put in.

RS

Kath Ferguson and husband, Ron.

'Partners'. A poem by Kath Ferguson of Hull.

> ### Partners
>
> As we walk through life, hand in hand
> Vowed to each other, till the promised land
> We know the road we will take
> Our marriage vows, the stronger will make
> To share each others fears and doubts
> Relying on each other, is what it's about
> As years go on and our children grow
> The love we have will continue to flow
> And as our book of life goes on
> There for us, one day to read
> The quality in love and need
> We've shared to great extent
> Has meant our years together,
> have been well spent
> So look back from time to time
> And thank God, for peace be thine
>
> 19 · 8 · 94

Housework

I let him do most the housework now – wash the windows. The only thing he won't do is iron. He can't wash 'cos he doesn't know how to work the machine. He doesn't know how to work the video!

MW

Poorly Man

Ron's been on a poorly man for many years so I'd got into that routine where I could go to work and it was like role reversal – where they say house-husbands now, well we were doing that before it was ever invented 'cos that was the situation. He was too ill to work so then I took on that role…I started as school meals…and I could take Paul who is now thirty-two. After that I started working at Hull Royal. Things were better then because you were on that regular wage. I was there during the day but Ron was there on a night-time for the kids. Because you had that settled wage you could organise yourself. It's all a different ball game now. It's like a 50:50 thing what you can do.

KF

Restless

He didn't like being home from sea that long. He was that used to going. After being home a week or two he got restless. But, he said, 'I'm enjoying my life here, you know.'

FW

CHAPTER 8

Community action

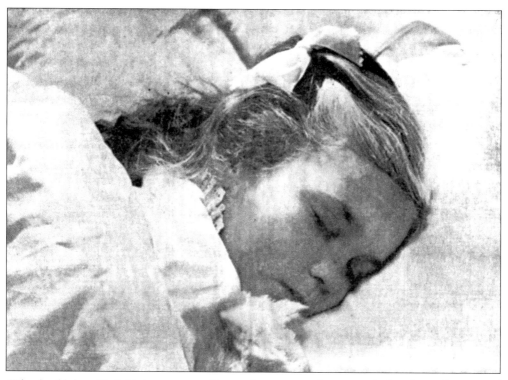

'Why should she suffer?' this image was used by trawler owners at the time of dock strikes in the spring of 1957.

Rita Stocks (back row, right) and Gwen Hallibone (back row, centre), with colleagues in the canteen.

The Heat is On

I remember one morning it was that cold, we all refused to come out the cloakroom and one of the lasses run to Riby Square...the union place...dodged out to Riby Square and fetched the union bloke. There was hell on. We got heaters then, but portable heaters.

GH

Is Archie in?

When Roy was fishing we had a shift rota. You did three nights overtime one week and you did two the next – that's how it worked. If I wanted time off when he came home and it was my shift to work I just used to go to the foreman and I used to say to him – he used to call him Archie – and he used to say, 'I bet Archie's in'. It was just something he used to say. And I used to say, 'Yeah, he is' and he used to say, 'No, you can't'. And I used to say, 'Well, I'm gonna do, anyway'. I used to say to him that if you let me have the two nights off, or whatever it was, I'll work all next week. And they would let you, if you asked.

MR

Smoke Break

We used to have five minutes smoke break. This charge hand

we had, kicked open the door. 'Come on. Let's have you'. 'We're not coming out'. Mind you, we was frightened to death. I think if one had got up and walked out, they'd have all. But, we stuck it out, 'cos it really used to be cold. You used to run to the cloakroom when it was your five minutes to try and get near the pipes. To sit near the pipes and get warm. As I say, I stuck it all them years.

GH

Stick Together

Well, all fishermen and their wives...they all stuck together – which you should at times like that. It's no good half pulling one way and the other half pulling another. Well, it didn't last long, a lot of them started giving in 'cos they were thinking of the money and the kids going without. 'Cos you couldn't live on the benefit. [The men] got bored. They wanted to get back to sea, 'cos after they'd been home so long they want to be back. I don't know why, 'cos it was awful.

DM

Immingham, one of the UK ports blockaded as part of the fishermen's national protest in 1974.

Fish Strike

I was with him on strike. There was a fish strike and that was hilarious because they had parties every night.

FW

Voicebox

There wouldn't have been no lumpers if there hadn't been fishermen, would there? You'd all the fish houses and everything was connected with the fish and yet, the lumpers got all that money when they packed up and the fishermen got nowt.

KF

Dig Deep

As you know, they're fighting for compensation now. As I say, a miner – I know it's a tough job and I don't disrespect it. But, a miner does go home to his wife every night, and his children. These men didn't. And, they (the miners), they only have to moan and groan and they get handouts for this and that and they get their money without any effort. These poor fishermen have been fighting twenty years to get redundancy money, which should have been paid. It was paid but it was paid to the trawler owners, fishermen never got nothing. And you see this is why they've been up to London again, on the protest march again – to try and get it sorted out. So, they should really pull their damn fingers out, this government and give them the money. 'Cos a lot of them have died. A lot of them still haven't got jobs. 'Cos they don't know anything else but fishing. How can you pen a man in a factory that's used to rolling fresh air and rolling in ships. You can't pen 'em in anywhere. That's why they can't stay in houses. They miss the roll of the sea.

MG

Turn a Blind Eye

I don't think it's fair. That's my point of view...I think it's a disgrace that this government can turn a blind eye on it all. Dollie Hardie, as you know, has been fighting a long, long while for this.

PW

Why Bother?

Well, the attitude with men is 'Why bother?' Which to me is the wrong attitude. I mean, if we all said that, like you and I, if I sat back in a chair and said 'why bother', what a mess we would be in. But, you see they didn't care. When they went on strike to get any extra money or get the job sorted out, they couldn't stick it, 'cos as soon as they offered them a copper or two to go to sea and gave them a pint of beer, they were off.

MG

Bye Bye

I sympathise greatly with those that lost their jobs and many lost their own ships as well. I don't think enough was done for them when it should of been done for them and actually, I think, further back better provisions should've been made for these fishermen by the trawler owners. Many worked for the same firm for year upon year upon year and of course there were no pensions when they came out – that was it. The boats get tied up or whatever and suddenly they say 'Bye-bye'. I dealt with over 1,500 (proxy payment) applications.

JM

Noses in the Dirt

Well, I mean, most the women were disgusted about it. I mean, they can find money for other things. When the war was on they used the fishermen and the fishermen's boats to help to fight a war. So, why rub their noses in the dirt? I was gonna swear then but I won't. But, I mean, why rub their noses in the dirt? And that's what this government is doing and yet, it's supposed to be for poor people. Well, who's poorer than the fishermen and his wife. They've always been poor people. If you didn't have the fish and you didn't hit the right market, you never had the money.

MG

Busy Doing Nothing

Something needs to be done because the situation is deteriorating from what I get to know. Somebody, somewhere has just got to listen to what they're saying. Not arriving in the port with a camera crew and saying, 'Oh yes, I support the fishermen's plight and I'm going to take this back to the House of Commons' and then doing nothing.

JM

Casual Work?

Well Dolly Hardie, bless her, she's the one that fought and actually got the redundancy, it was a seventeen-year battle and she proved that fishermen were not casual workers…having been made redundant by the firm saying we are tying your ship up, we are finishing, they should at that time, like other workers, have had three months severance pay, they could not have that as they were classed as casual. They should have had compensation for the loss of their employment because the firms were closing down, they couldn't have that and what did he end up with? Fourteen and a half years in Wyre trawlers and another year and a half? I got £1,900 pounds for that time for ex-gratia redundancy, they paid us interest at six per cent for every year. It was simple interest so I ended up with just short of £4,000. They'd paid into pension schemes and as soon as skippers and mates had paid into pension schemes and they were told if they did not take the pension schemes that was offered by the company they would find

Fishermen's protest march, 30 May 1980.

a different skipper or mate or crew. When they closed the firms down…those pensions – they give them back what they paid in. These pensions they shouldn't have paid that money back to the men at that time, I mean they paid one £98 back and what can you do with £98? The best paid skipper got paid £400 I had to tell Dolly, it could have been her husband that got it, but can you make it perfectly clear to these guys in parliament that the £400 was for the whole time, not £400 a week like they would obviously think. I am the secretary of the British Fishermen's Association and when we call an Annual General Meeting they are very reluctant to come out, they don't want to. If I put it in the paper that there is some money to be dished out, I would say you would get a couple of hundred fellas turn up, but there is a sort of apathy, they have lost hope. If you get fifteen there you are lucky.

PW

Dig in Your Pockets

I think the fishermen were robbed. Like when they had that strike I was at the front of the strike. That was going back years. I forget what year that is. They put me at the front 'cos I had a couple of kids in the pram, you see the rest would be at school. They said, 'Oh, we're going to put you here'. I said, 'Why?' They said, 'Oh, 'cos we like your slogan'. I put, 'Dig in your pockets and

100

pay out of the profits'. I went all the way down Dock Street and all up Lord Street with this slogan on the pram and they said, 'That's a good one'. Not that it did very good, I don't think we got much more after that. There were quite a lot of women involved with it. They used to go to these meetings. Well, if you could get there. If you had somebody to look after the children – you had to pay somebody. Well, we didn't get a lot of money to fork it out.

DM

Fish Supper

They treated the fishermen as if they're dirt under their feet. I mean I don't know how they can sit – these in the Houses of Parliament – sit down and eat a nice piece of fish. Doing what they're doing to the fishermen They've not been out to see how hard it is. They always used to say about the miners, but they had a back door. They had no chance, whatsoever. To me, they've been treated utterly wrong, they have, really. They've been treated like dirt really. It's a shame – they couldn't care less. They think they're just a number.

CS

Golden Handshake

My husband had men go to sea with him that couldn't even stand up properly on deck. They couldn't do a day's work and yet they ended up going to work in ICI as labourers and ended up with massive pensions and £30,000

golden handshakes. You know, these are things that really grip you. What did we do wrong?

PW

Bash Him

We're now looking to the government to fulfil the promises that they made to the fishermen in the 1979 manifesto. I mean John Prescott's another one that we are going to have a go at. He said 'Why treat the fishermen like this – they were treated with vicious and antiquated business methods'. He's always saying 'Don't let the fishermen down'. So I think Dolly's (Hardie) gonna bash him! You do think you're making a nuisance of yourself but it's the only way you'll get somewhere'. I know the life fishermen have led and their families and I do think that they deserve to have decent retirements. When they started arguing about the ships, you know the flagship skippers, they said as long as they had, I think, 75% Common Market crew. So they had British fishermen going out there so I used to get them. I mean I was once in Spain, I went over to visit Ron while he was fishing out of Spain and they took me in the boardroom to meet the boss and the boss said, 'We need two deck hands for this ship'. One said 'We've got a number in Fleetwood we ring and she will get deck hands for us', and I'm sitting there and I said, 'What number are you ringing?' and it was me they were trying to get!

PW

Dolly Hardie addresses a meeting of more than 1,000 ex-fishermen and their families at the ice house. (*Grimsby Evening Telegraph*, 11 December 1993)

Carry the Worry

I am a very placid person, I tear strips off myself inside, I'm known for that, but people say outwardly I look calm. I developed asthma anyway, I think that was all part and parcel of it…tension…they tell me I'm a chronic hypertensive. You carry the worries inside you because you can't let them see…I mean he'd be worried about you and I think if you can sort of pretend everything's okay and that you're coping.

PW

Pen to Paper

Then there was a miner's wife and I thought 'Well, we have lived as hard as miner's wives'. At least they go home at night and they do see 'em every night. I know it's a hard life being down below. So I just put pen to paper when all those ships was lost. They (*Women's Own*) wrote and said it was a good story. It was the way we lived.

EM

Skipper's Ticket

When he was mate and we bought this house he had sciatica in his leg so we decided the best thing to do, because we had a baby then, was to get his skipper's ticket and I used to sit with him and go through his articles with him. Oh it was dreadful. I think I could of took a ticket! He took his ticket, you used to get £2.50 a week off the White Fish Authority to live off, that's all you got while they were taking the ticket.

PW

Big Lil

I can remember Lilly Billocca going up and down Hessle Road. [My mother] didn't really agree with her because ladies didn't behave like that. She would turn her off if she came on the telly. I don't think she understood all that she was campaigning for. To me mother that was a way of life and that's what you did. Because fishermen's wives weren't really like that in my mother's book – which, I suppose they weren't. I

ian Bilocca answers her critics at the fishermen's wives' meeting at the Central imsby, last night. Making sure the meeting is kept in order are (left to right) Hall, Transport and General Workers' Union Grimsby fishing organ'ser; Mr. ms, TGWU Grimsby district secretary; and Mrs. Vera Tidswell-Howard (right.)

erator on the Notts. County, Mr. Herbert Joys, puts over a few points at the meeting.

Angry scenes—but Big Lil wins the day

ANGRY SCENES erupted last night when Mrs. Lilian Bilocca appealed to 150 Grimsby fishermen's wives to support her campaign for greater safety on board trawlers.

Union officials made several attempts to call the gathering to order and it was not until they threatened to close down the meeting that the shouting stopped.

Several people, including wives who had lost relatives at sea and Mr. Herbert Joys, radio operator on the stranded trawler Notts County, protested to Mrs. Bilocca and Mrs. Vera Tidswell-Howard, leader of the Grimsby wives' protest The women were told to leave the fight for safety to the men.

But the two campaigners finally won the day and were cheered as they outlined their plans for better conditions at sea.

As "Big Lil" and her supporters left Grimsby Central Hall for Hull they were besieged by autograph hunters and questioned by anxious women.

batters against our windows, we are thinking of our husbands and wondering if they are safe."

She said that she had been told to stay at home and do her knitting, but it was the right of fishermen's wives to air their views, especially where safety was concerned

Mrs. Tidswell - Howard went on : " Our men have to work hard. They have to work round the clock, and there is no overtime. They live in cramped and uncomfortable conditions. Can you imagine what it is like when there is a gale blowing ? There is not a moment's peace, and they are not able to rest for a second."

Lilian Bilocca's appeal to fishermen's wives to support the campaign for greater safety on board trawlers, *Grimsby Evening Telegraph*, 14 July 1968.

think there was a lot of support [for her] from the younger people but certainly not from my mother 'cos she was from an older generation. I think in lots of ways she understood what she was doing, but didn't think that was the way…end of story. She didn't think it was right – didn't think it was ladylike. But, I mean, she wouldn't go to any meetings with Lilly Billocca there.

VS

Your Next Penny

The thing is I've been there. As a skipper's wife and a skipper's daughter you, perhaps, lose contact but then when you see it hit you and everything goes, you realise then. This was about a week before Christmas one year…I used to go and order the food for the boat so I thought 'Well I'll get enough food for us and charge it to the boat'. I know what it's like to [not] know where your next penny's coming from and I can see other people now in the town and I know they're in that state. I help people now fill in forms for anything to do with Social Services…they don't bother to claim what they should.

PW

City Challenge

You could see it gradually happening, I think. My son died last year, he was twenty-six, he died of a drugs overdose. I had four children, he was the only one that went wrong. All his age group it seemed, at that time went into joy riding. I'd see burnt out cars on the estate. You'd phone the police and you'd two big families on the estate and people were frightened of reporting crime. It just got terrible by the day. It was gradual. I'd lived here all my life and I've had all the problems, if not more than, any resident could have here. It was after the riots, I've worked on machines all my life and I thought 'I'm gonna go back to college' and I wanted to become a probation officer and they said 'You need to do some therapy work'. So I started doing therapy work on the estate. I've lived here all my life and I didn't realise things had got so bad. I didn't realise the problems that people were living – I thought it was just me who had these problems and I wasn't unique everybody had some kind of problems. So I just started up with pressure groups that were trying to get things changed on the estate for the better and I'm still here. We got City Challenge money going into it [the community centre]. The lads who built it were actually in the riots. There's nine of them that formed their own construction company. Every one had a criminal record and they formed their own company…they built this and they built the building at the back of here and they also built the bungalows on the estate so that was an achievement in itself.

CB

CHAPTER 9

Work

Women at work. Herring lasses
in the late nineteenth century.
'Following the fishing' went into
decline following the Second
World War.

'There's a thousand landing'. Working on Grimsby fish docks, 1961.

Joy of Work

It was a joy to go to work. Some people, they have work and they hate it, don't they? But, it was nice, I liked going there even though it was a little old place. There was one part where you used to wrap the packs of fish and there was holes in the ceiling and if rained the rain come in, and if it snowed, the snow come. It was that cold, we used to have portable heaters, you know, to keep you warm and that. But, as I say, I liked it there.

GH

On Broadway

So, I rung me mother up. 'Oh, yeah', she said, 'You can come back. He isn't coming back'. I said, 'No, only me and the [child] Pat'. She said, 'Yes'. So I packed everything in the bloody pram again, goes back to Broadway again and I had to go out to work. She said I had to pay me lodge. She said, 'No, no. You have to work. I'll look after her through…get a part-time job'. So, I went braiding, but, you see, even then uncle come downstairs one morning and I was still stood there at three o'clock in the snow, wrapped up in a big sea jersey, still making me money up.

MG

Fish out of Water

Well, when I first went out in the canteen, I felt like a fish out of water – 'cos I'd never done canteen

Northern Trawlers' net room, c. 1960.

work before. But then, I liked it in the end. It was warmer. Let's face it. I was in the warm. It was cold in the factory. You couldn't have it really warm. When I first started at Orwell Street you never had gloves or anything like that. You bought your own overalls, your own wellingtons, your own socks. You bought everything. It was always cold. I've stood there cutting portions and when it's time to go for a break, me feet's been like two stumps, I could hardly walk away. But, as I say, I liked it. I wouldn't have stood there all them years if I hadn't of liked it.

GH

Nautical School

It was all the drink. So, I really had had enough by then so I thought, 'I'll take on another job'. So I did. And I became head (domestic) of the Nautical School, as the only woman among eight hundred men. The only woman that looked after them, cleaned for them, looked after the boys – the apprentice boys – even the Navy when they came. Until I retired, but I still carried on with me papering and I still paper today.

MG

Every House in Town

You got a good laugh and there was all different types of people but there was lots of them that was either courting or married to fishermen. 'Cos this is what this town consisted of. Every family had something to do with the fishing industry. Whether it be a shipwright or filleter or packer or smoker. Anything like that. Nearly every house in the town had something to do with it.

MR

Old Fish Houses

You had an hour for dinner. Finished at twelve and went back at one. And, say, you come out, finished at twelve, and thought, 'Ooh, I'm not going back there. Don't like it'. You could start work at one o'clock in another factory. 'Cos they was so close together. Down Riby Street, there was

factories close together…what you call the old fish houses.

GH

Walking on Sponge

Oh! Cold! In the winter it was freezing. We used to have bowls with red hot water in, but within seconds it used to be stone cold because your hands were that cold – and your feet. And you wore wellingtons with hob socks, but, you know, your feet and your hands used to be freezing, they did. You used to walk about like you was walking on sponge. You couldn't feel your feet, you know. Everybody you looked at used to be blue.

MR

Cod War

Then, obviously, the Cod War affected every port but Fleetwood a lot more than a lot of the other ports. The mission had a hostel here and a café here and the mission chapel. So the mission, in London, decided, because of the decline in the fishing industry, that it was obviously not financially viable to keep a big centre going because the role of the fisherman's mission in the port of Fleetwood had to change. So, I came for a month and a month became two months and two months became three months and suddenly I was asked to stay…six years ago. Of course publicity wise I had a tremendous amount of coverage because first of all, I was known in the town, I know a lot of people. And secondly, apart from the war, I was the only, I *am* the only woman to run a centre – it's all run by a man, you see. So I expected vast opposition from, you know, some in the mission – I didn't get it. I think a few looked and thought what the hell was the mission playing at but they've all been very supportive. So, I got support from day one and of course I tried, the best way I could, to inject a new approach to the work here and it was either going to work or London was going to say you haven't made it work so that's it. I wanted to prove that there was a need for a mission presence in Fleetwood. A lot just identified the mission as a chap in a uniform and a peak cap going and knocking on a door when somebody dies…talking, sitting in a room with a widow.

JM

A *Thousand Landing*

You used to look in the paper on a Monday night and say, 'Oh, hell look at all that fish. There's a thousand landing'. I mean that was hell of a lot of fish. I mean, it was the main fishing port – Grimsby – then. Me mother worked amongst the fish, before she was married. She started work at thirteen and she worked in the old fish houses when you went in a morning, breaking the ice off the tubs. She said the women used to be fainting with the cold and that. But, she enjoyed it as well, and

Midnight millionaires. Lumpers at work in the late 1940s.

Packing filleted fish as part of the fishcake production plant, 1959.

when she got married she had six children and that was it – she never went to work anymore – she couldn't go to work anymore.

GH

Woman on a Mission

We are dealing solely with retired fishermen that got the bad deal in the Cod War that were in jobs in Marr's, in Ross, in Wyre, all these big firms. If a fisherman that is still sailing came in and wanted his records or wanted details about the prospect of finishing going to sea, they'll come in as a general enquiry but the main part of the welfare job is looking after and

giving welfare advice to all the ex-fishermen.

JM

Side Splitting

I left school at fifteen and worked at John L. Greens on the fish dock, I started there as a briner you know working in the briner with the haddock and went on the melts machine, which was a horrible job, you sat on the machine and put herrings though and they split their guts open and you got all these smells outside and you used to pick them up with your hands and your hands used to be all gooey.

RS

Messing About

Ena always got her work done a day or two days before and she would have extra work and she would have that done on the Wednesday but saying that, me, I was a mess-abouter. I mean I would make the girls laugh and take people off. The old forewoman she was massive and she used to walk like that you know and I used to take her off and things…I did not care in them days.

JH

Break Time

Down dock it used to be so cold. It was freezing. You used to be feeding the herring machine…it was all go but I enjoyed it. I was busy, something to do. Well, after that we used to have a bit of a sing-song. When it was our break time we used to run across to Solly's and get a muffin bun and come back…a muffin bun and sit and eat a kipper. You'd see the grease – you wouldn't believe it – but, oh, they was beautiful.

NG

Public Information

At times I've got to be very, very hard with some of these people because, as I say, they think the world owes them a favour. In a lot of cases, the world does or somebody does. In a lot it is not, I would say, ignorance but they just haven't been informed enough about what is available…attendance allowance…Invalidity pension…Income support…Rent and rate relief.

JM

Cod Heads

If you went on the bike, which I did later on when I had earned the money to buy one, you used to go down Cleethorpes Road, turn in Riby Square

June Hewitt, the 'mess-abouter'.

Colbridges cod liver oil company, Grimsby, at the turn of the century.

and round onto the dock along the pontoon with the fish train dripping smelly water cod heads all over to work. It was nice, it was alright I enjoyed it!

JH

Ice Cream Man

I mean I even set to in an ice cream kiosk. And the funny thing was whilst he was running the boat some days he'd come off the boat and he'd come up – you could tell he was always covered in oil – scrubbed himself all over. And he'd say, 'You go away, love, go on, I'll serve for you'. This is a bit cruel really – and I'd come back and he'd closed up and he'd took my takings to go in the bowling green with! So, what could you say about that?

PW

Favourites

You used to have nice overalls and hats and that. Whereas when you worked in the old factories you was glad of wearing a polo neck jumper to keep you warm. I think when we moved in the new factories, you find a lot of bickering with the women. You had little groups of women. When you was on the briner it was very rare that the men was on that, they was all filleting, so of course the men was all friendly. Well, of course, men were on high wages in the older days but in the new factories it was brought up to equal pay. It was mainly all men. It wasn't till we got to Findus that you got the women supervisors. Well, with women, they always had their favourite ones, where when we in the old factories they treat you all the same.

RS

Off Their Butts!

I'm sorry, I don't suffer fools gladly. I will help anyone that walks through that door that I think is genuine but if some guy comes in there and says 'Oh, I've had nothing all my life', it's the government to blame for this or it's his mother to blame or it was his wife to blame for it…they're quite capable of getting off their butts and doing something constructive with their lives.

JM

House Husband

He was not so bothered when I first started, but when I got made supervisor and went days and had to work twelve hours a day, he used to moan a bit then because he use to be at work at six in the morning till six at night and he did not get home till half six, quarter to seven at night, so he used to spend a bit of time on his own. He was good, he used to do the tea for us and washing, but he said it was too many hours really for a woman.

RS

Mother's Footsteps

When my dad had his accident at sea…she couldn't go out to work because of the children. So she took in doing home braiding and she used to do a lot for Middletons. They used to deliver twine to the house. You had to do

Cosalt Fishing Gear, Grimsby.

The old fashioned way. Fish are prepared for curing.

belly tops, squares and wings and all that. Me sister used to like braiding an' all and she used to be helping her and there was me sat filling needles. We've done it while one and two in the morning. I got into it and after I lost Albert myself, later on in life, I decided to take it up meself and the same company delivered to me what used to be delivered to me mum. Down my hallway I used to tie these loops in the pieces of rope and put them over the cupboard door, then shut the door and sneck it and then have me pole across and I used to be braiding away there and the next thing, the woman next door started complaining – said she could hear a clicking noise. It was just because I was earning a bit of money and she wasn't and so that put the tin hat on that.

NG

Finger Work

As you were filling they learnt you, when they got a few minutes, how to braid and you used to bring samples home when you'd been doing it six to nine months. I took one home and I couldn't remember and Uncle Bob used to go to sea...I said to him 'How do you this, Uncle Bob?' He did it with fingers, not the spool, 'Course, I started doing it with fingers and when I took it in next morning the forewoman said, 'Who the hell done this? It's all shapes and sizes'. Well, I said my Uncle Bob showed me, so she said 'Is he a fisherman? It's no good.'

JH

High Class

When you compare some of the prostitutes now to what they were, there were some high class prostitutes. They really would sit and have a talk to you and enjoy themselves. It was a way of life that you would have to live through to realise.

KF

Crawling Back

I really enjoyed it. They got this enormous machine called the rackie. I was the one woman that got the job of cleaning it and you had to clean every bit by hand. You used to go inside the big freezers on a Sunday night and clean them all down. You used to have to crawl under these bars. Make sure all the walls was clean. Anyway, I got pulled up by one of the charge hands one day, and he said, 'Norma, You've let me down!' And I said, 'Pardon?' 'You've let me down.' I said, 'What for?' He said, 'Just look at this machine. It's crawling.' I looked and there was all maggots on it. 'Erm, who was doing this job last week?', and he went, 'You, of course!' I said, 'I've just come back after a two week holiday'. And the manager said, 'I knew this wasn't her work. Now, you apologise to her' and he went. 'Umm, umm. I'm sorry. I'm sorry'.

NG

Big Sis

We had a prostitute at the top of the terrace. She was known as Big Sis. She used to wear all these big, big hats. A very tall and smart woman. I mean, you knew she brought all these people home but you didn't actually know the term, the terminology for a prostitute. If she was on a bad run – everything went to the pawn shop which was Izzy Turners on Hessle Road.

KF

In His Shoes

When she was young she used to work in a fish house – and she used to go with men's boots on. And her sister used to work there and me mum's sister wouldn't wear these men's boots and used to go in bare feet. She died – she got rheumatoid arthritis.

OL

Sidelines

Women were on the sidelines, as it were. In the fish houses and the wet fish shop or the braiders. One lady down Bean Street would take the bags to wash for a lot of the women to earn her money and in-between she used to net braid and she had a broom handle where there had been shutters on the window. They had the hooks and they used to put the broom handle on there and she used to net and she used to have her own pram and she used to take it down dock. She did this at home outside but she also used to take a lot of the fishermen's bags for the wives. Remember, if they were going back on that ship a lot of them didn't have two bags. Some did who was pretty well off, but others had to have that bag done and dried ready in two days, she was forever up at half past four standing in the queue down Regents Street for the wash house.

KF

Family Credit

Most of the jobs are just twenty hour posts. Most people are better off staying on the dole than going into work but single parents who can do the twenty hours and get that family credit…I mean there's plenty of these kind of jobs. This estate has been predominantly women led. You know, the men just lost interest. It must be horrible for men to see that their wives can get a job and they can go to work and now the wife's taken over the role that the man's always had. I mean that must be a terrible blow to a man's confidence that the woman's now the boss…Years ago it was the man that was always the boss. My next door neighbour, he's got two kids and he wants to go to work. He's at the dole every day. He's just a casual worker on the fish quay and all the jobs they offer him makes him worse off coming off the dole. But for the majority of men, if they're with their partners, to come off benefit they need quite a good wage and them wages aren't around. Not for unskilled people.

CB

Chance in a Million

When we was fish washing the men used to head it and we used to gather it on a big slab and used to get three big barrels…three each, there were three fish washers to a tub. You put some hot water in first and then put cold into it to run it off. But if there were no hot water in the winter you used to wash it in cold water with all the ice on top and you had to do three barrels each. And you had linen finger stalls…you got the knife, cut it down and crack the bone at the bottom. Pull the knife up so all the black and everything was up. Well, all that went in the water, you see. Then when everybody had done their three kegs we pulled the plug. The water came out and then we went on bonus. And you had to do nine barrels before you could pull the plug to let fresh water in every time. There used to be three washers. There used to be a woman on the other side. There was a splitter and they could only cut a certain way and if they didn't do it perfect, that haddock was out. If you didn't cut your fish properly for fish washing, that was out. Everything had to be perfect cut. The splitter…every so often got a big knife, put it under all of them and put them on big trays and then they went to clear brines…no colouring or anything. They was on about fifteen minutes then they'd go on what you called a wooden horse and when they was all ready somebody else used to put them in the smoke house.

And when they was cured they used to have a dry part and they used to do all the packing, and you didn't see them anymore but when it was break time on the morning someone used to go for all

Top and tailing. Splitting the fish ready for salting.

the teas at Solly's café and bread buns and we used to pinch kippers to go in these buns for our break. Then you didn't get no more break till dinner, then you got an hour. You could go home or stay there. And then, on the afternoon you got a mug of tea – you paid for your own, like – and went and stood at the tub while he was working. They expected you to work overtime. You had to have a real good excuse to get out of it. Like meeting a millionaire! Well, we never met many millionaires down dock, so that didn't wash!

DW

Empty Home

I'd always arranged that when he was coming in from sea I could have me days off. One of the other girls would always swap with me. Because men don't like coming home to an empty house – especially fishermen. And them days, they were only in two days. They were no sooner in and they were going back again.

AS

Sick of Fish

When they brought the fish into the fish house it made you sick 'cos there was that much and you knew what your day of work would be.

MW

Lots of Laughs

Mind you, a lot of people thought them days were all work, but we had a lot of laughs…you used to look forward to going to work and you used to think I'll wait for so-and-so and there'd be a load of filleters there and they'd come and chat you up. If there weren't a lot of work at John L. Greens, we'd maybe work two hours, they'd send us home and they'd expect you to go back at nights and you just did it.

DW

Happy Days

They were the happiest days of my life at Findus.

RS

Perks

There was none of that sexual harassment. We just thought it was one of the perks of the job.

MW

Plod and Plonk

We used to meet the plonkies and the police…they used to pop in and see us and we often used to give them a cup of tea.

DW

Slave Labour

It's always women doing the braiding. Never men…it was never good

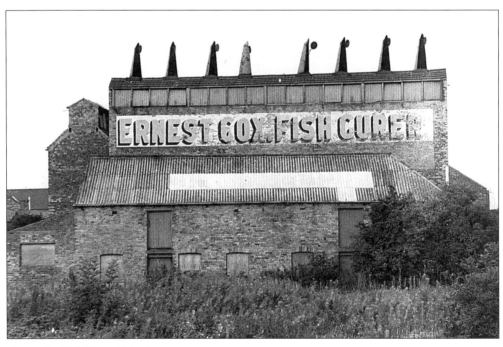

Ernest Cox Fish Curer, Grimsby.

Cosalt braiding room, c. 1910.

money…they used to call it slave money.

VJ

A Bit Faint

I was desperate to have one night off, Maggie Sparks said, 'Go upstairs and pretend to faint'. I goes upstairs and of course I was looking round to see…and I just bobbed down on the floor and Maggie says, 'Ooh, come and look! There's something wrong with Rita'. Anyway, she come and I started laughing and she said, 'Shurrup. Eric's coming'. Anyway, he says, 'You'd better go home if you're not very well'.

RS

Terms and Conditions

I f they opened a factory for old people I'd definitely go back to work there – if there was men there.

DW

For Better or Worse

B raiding just dropped off. They made us all redundant…we don't do it for fishing now. There isn't no ships. There's only about twelve braiders left in Grimsby now. Years ago when you first started you used to have blisters on your hands…I had blisters on both hands…but now it's all 100% better.

VJ

Demolition of Riby Street fish house, Grimsby, 1969.

Misunderstood

It was good, yes if you worked in a fish house. An' they used to say fishwives…but, all the lasses wasn't like that. You got the odd ones that used to show their ignorance but, it was just they used to say – you know – fishwife, if you worked in a fish house. But as I say, nice people worked in them.

MR

Send Off

You can tell how well thought of I was at Ross's. I never saw a send off like it in my life. You usually get £20 for each year you've worked there. I got £400 – which got my gold watch. Anyhow, when I went in on my last night I went, 'Oh, no' and in the corridor over the clock there was these big banners, they said, 'Happy Retirement, Norma'. Well, I goes into the canteen, the table there was laid for a buffet and there was another big banner. I hadn't got to do no work the last night. I'd got to go round the factory and say cheerio to them all. I was choked at the table. Couldn't open the box…tears streaming down.

NG

CHAPTER 10
Postscript

A lone seagull.

Years On

Even now, after doing all those years on nights I can't sleep properly. I get up and do me housework at night.

NG

What Now?

There's no fishing. There's no nothing.

EM

Downhill

I think everything's gone downhill since the fishing industry's finished. You know, I mean look at all the shops. I mean, any day of the week you could go down Freeman Street, whether you was shopping, or whatever it was you were doing. And it was just alive with people. I mean, it's like a ghost town now, isn't it? But, there was so many boats came in a day, as well, so there was always men and wives flitting from pub to pub, shopping and what-have-you.

MR

Moving On

Well, they pulled all the houses down around there and we got a council house. You see, they wanted all the land round there for the new factories that've gone up, and different things and all that. Mind you, it's just that we've…you've bettered yourself by moving. I mean, they was old houses with no gardens or anything, they never had. They was straight out onto the street. So, I think, you bettered yourself as you went along. But, as I say, if they want the land they'll take it, won't they?

GH

Neighbours

I always think that life goes on, doesn't it? It's got to, hasn't it? But it's that neighbourly thing 'cos now neighbours don't know a neighbour, do they? Or anything. It's like when we lived in Weelsby Street before we moved here. I lived there for twenty-eight year – and you slowly see it as each old neighbour moved out and new ones moved in, that's when it seemed like that they started keeping themselves to themselves. They wasn't bothered about if the lady next door was poorly or anything like that. Now, I'm still like that. If I thought that anybody was poorly – like when one of my neighbours was poorly – got children or if any of the bairns was poorly – I'd knock. I'd say does anyone want anything bringing from the shops. I would round here. Even though I don't know them, a lot. But, that's how it made you in them days. You know, you was always ready to give your help to somebody. But, they seem to have lost it all now, don't they?

MR

The dock was like a town on its own, Northwall, Grimsby, in the 1950s.

Walking the Streets

They'd help each other, whereas now, people are a bit aloof...They don't mix like they used to...You could go out and leave the door open. I could walk the streets. I mean, when I was single and lived over the Marsh area. There was the trams running. They used to bring the foreigners and they used to sit in this, like a little station it was…and wait for the tram. Well you could walk past there at ten on a night, say coming from the pictures and they didn't say a word to you. But, nowadays – I wouldn't dare.

GH

Wear and Tear

I liked every job I had. I liked braiding. I liked post work. I liked the post round and everything. I got quite used to it. And of course I liked the papering, and I used to like it when I took the samples of carpets round. And when I did the leaflets I used to have eight women. In charge of eight women doing four lots of leaflets all round Lincolnshire. Take them all in the car, and everything…I'm sitting here now resting. I'm only resting. Bur normally, I'll be trying to rush round doing. I can't because I'm full of arthritis. Or as my doctor says – hard wear and tear. This is what he's said – you've worked too hard. I mean, I'm doctoring all the time. I'm on pills all the time. But, I mean, that doesn't stop me doing.

MG

123

Under the Thumb

A lot of people used to say…like my girls will say, 'You're under the thumb, mother. I'm not gonna be'. Now they look at it in a different light, but that was how it was done then. Like I said, in some respects they're in the right and I'm in the right. Well, it always seemed that it was a man's world then. We seemed to take more then. You seemed like…whatever they said was right. I wouldn't take anything now. Like, as I say, as you get older you learn.

MR

Handouts

This is a bugbear with me. When I was having trouble trying to keep my children and no money – because my husband had sloped off. No social services helped me. They never gave me a crust of bread. And yet, I'd three children. Today, if your husband walks out the door, they run and get social security and they give 'em houses and look after the children and make sure they're all right. Today, nobody helps me. I'm still paying taxes on my bit of savings. Only what I've worked for. No handouts whatsoever. So, that's my grievance.

MG

Blossoming

He was sixty-seven when he died so she'd be about sixty-three, sixty-four and then she sort of blossomed – at that age. She found it very difficult to do it at first. I always found that amusing – 'cos she always thought my dad was watching her and wouldn't like the way she was spending his money. Not that he left an awful lot but for the first time in her life everything that came into the house was hers.

VS

All Pull Together

As I've always said as far as Fleetwood people goes, they pull together in Fleetwood. You knock one and they all limp in Fleetwood and that's how it is a very close-knit community. They all try and help each other. I don't think any of them have been down for long. Very despondent, very disheartened but they all try and strive to pull together.

JM

Hessle Road

I've nothing against Hessle Road, because I think it's being born there and living there that's made us all what we are today. And I believe it's due to all that, you know. Due to the strictness of the upbringing, to the respect that we had for our parents. I wouldn't of had it any other way. I'm just sorry to a lesser extent that it doesn't go on today. I've got all three brothers and all three sisters and we don't live in each other's pockets, but you've only to pick up the phone and there's somebody there. The families that I knew were like that.

VS

124

Nowt Good

There was nowt good about the life. I didn't think so. There was nowt good about it.

MG

Before Her Time

She always had people to clean for her, I know that. She was a bit of a snob, I suppose. No, I suppose that's a bit unfair. I don't know what she was. I do know she was very strong and I always felt she was before her time, because now you'd make your daughters have a career, wouldn't you, and go to university and things like that. Well, she thought about that. Years ago.

VS

Cameraderie

You were safer walking home as well when we were teenagers. There wasn't all this worry. Maybe, there was rapists out there, I don't know, but you never heard of anything like this. But you could walk home with your friends at one or two in the morning from the dancing and know you were safe. You were really close to each other as friends as well. It was such a close community you lived with your friends as well. I don't think there's that comradeship – camaraderie – what there used to be. You walked in the community and you was safe, I mean, you never heard of anyone being mugged. You'd see the fights between the fellas or owt like that, but you never heard of anyone getting mugged. If they were beaten it was because they'd been in a fight and had too much to drink.

KF

Changes

It's not just changed here, it's changed in every port I would have thought. Especially Grimsby, Hull – those I've been connected with because at one time Fleetwood was the fishing industry, that's it. At school there was fathers who worked on the dock who were lumpers or had their own businesses and everything else. Then all of a sudden everything changed. The skippers dressed up with their wives, respected members of the community. Of course all the local pubs would be full. The shops thrived because fishermen were known as three-day millionaires. When I was taking my, as it was then, GCE, I worked in a jewellers in Fleetwood and we always knew when the ships were landing and the chappie that had the jewellers shop he said, 'It'll be very busy, very very busy on Thursday'. True to his word, you know, these fishermen would come in and be buying their wives earrings and bracelets and watches and everything else. So, yes these shops must've felt it. There wasn't the money being generated into the town. It's not just the ships tied up it's all those industries connected with fishing. The rope makers, the engineers, the painters, the ice companies. Even for the provisions on board the ship. All those sort of things so it's a knock on effect.

JM

125

Getting Better?

Ron said about three days before he died he said '…things will get better for you' and I never believed him at the time…I just wish Ron was here to share them.

PW

Starting Over

She [mother] travelled all over after my father died, she went holidaying. She felt quite guilty about that. We took her to the doctors and he said it was because she'd spent so many years being under the thumb and having to do as she was told. When he died, she had the freedom that she'd never had since…1926, 1925 she married. He died in '67 – that's forty-odd years – it's a long time, isn't it? Where she was virtually doing – most of the time – what she was told.

VS

A Great Shame

It was an honourable profession. The men that went to sea were largely brave, extremely hard working and honourable men. As in any walk of life you'd get the odd black sheep and there were drunkards, but there were men of high integrity. I knew men of great integrity and it's a great shame that the fishing industry has been allowed to go to develop or under develop the way it has during the last twenty-five years.

FWo

Community Spirit

They've just taken on a new lady with the council. She's trying to regenerate, plan what Fleetwood will be like but at the end of the day, you've got to give those people work. You know, you can't regenerate anything without somebody working. If you go around Fleetwood at tea time, after tea, it's dead. There is nothing, there is nothing…the harbour village has done very well but the heart of the town, there's a lot to be desired. I do think there's a lot of deterioration in the community spirit because I think people are watching their neighbours and wondering.

PW

Changing Prospects

Such as us – the back end streets, as we used to call it. I think we were expected to go into the fish houses. Now they're leaving school and going to colleges and what have you.

RS

Turn Back Time

If I had my life again I'd never marry a fisherman again – never. Oh no.

MG

Taking Charge

I now know that I was in charge of my life from being twelve years old because mum had lost interest in us and if I didn't wash my knickers, I didn't have a pair of knickers and launderettes started and I just thought how wonderful these are because I could regularly take my washing to get done because it used to stay in the pile for ages before it ever got done. I mean this sounds as though, you know, you've had a bloody awful life and looking back on it I know that I did, but it's made me what I am today which I find quite sad actually because there are certain things that I missed out on – I resent them, God I resent them.

LS

Missing Out?

People say about the hard life of the fishermen and what you never had, as a wife of a fisherman, you never missed.

PW

You Made Your Bed

Well, as I say, the two lads went to sea. Now they take a drink but they're not violent or anything. The fishing today is different. They accept that when they come ashore and they're married that they have to behave, because women today don't stand for it. Well, you know what I'm talking about. They don't stand for anything today. Women go off if the man looks the other way – they're out the door, aren't they. But, you see, I was brought up to stick. You made your bed, you laid on it. No help from your parents – you'd made your bed – you had to get on with it.

MG

It's Coming Back

From me growing up here it went really downhill. Horrible, really horrible but now, I would defy anyone that walks in them streets, it's changing. When I first started working here I organised a garden competition. This year, we're inundated, you've got to walk around and spot the bad garden now. I mean four year ago there wasn't a nice garden! That is people moving on it's coming back. Even putting the courses on. We could put on twice as many on as we do and all the tutors will say, 'They're an excellent group, they're so hungry to learn'. I do think that they've took pride in their community again. I find it difficult now to remember the state this estate was in.

CB

Stress and Strain

It was very rough, it wasn't all rosy. It was very rough and I would say that a lot of the women that turned to drink was because of how rough it was. The stress – others like me would have your depression and did not know what was wrong with you because of this depression, and what it was, was all the stress and strain, but it was not identified as it is now. There is a lot of things that have

North Shields fish quay, February 1990.

come out for the good nowadays.

KF

As It Was

I just look back and think they may have had a hard time, the women may have had a hard time, but they also had the good times. I suppose it would depend on who you were married to. All the time me dad was earning good money, we got it. We had holidays. He sent us all to Withernsea, and it was a bungalow... we had a pony and trap... When he came home from sea he came to Withernsea to be with us all. It was hard I suppose, but that was life and you didn't know any different. Looking back over my childhood I wouldn't have wanted another childhood. I don't know anybody that I would have changed my childhood with. Because I think it was a special community, on it's own.

VS

Talk Things Out

Sadly, as the fishing industry declines, more members of the fishing community will be coming to us for help. It's as simple as that. They'll come to the mission whereas they won't go to Citizen's Advice, they won't go to DSS but they'll come and talk things out with me here.

JM

Same Again

I think sometimes, 'Would I do it again?' And I would do it again. I'd go through it all again.

AS

Breaking the Mould

I think it broke the community up, actually. The pubs weren't the same, you know, the meeting places weren't the same. It's an era I don't think – if you need to create it – you could ever create it again.

KF